I HAVE RESOLVED NOT TO STOP

RANA PRATAP BAJAJ
ADITI SETHI

BLUEROSE PUBLISHERS
India | U.K.

Copyright © Rana Pratap Bajaj, Aditi Sethi 2023

All rights reserved by author. No part of this publication may be reproduced, stored in a retrieval system or transmitted in any form or by any means, electronic, mechanical, photocopying, recording or otherwise, without the prior permission of the author. Although every precaution has been taken to verify the accuracy of the information contained herein, the publisher assumes no responsibility for any errors or omissions. No liability is assumed for damages that may result from the use of information contained within.

BlueRose Publishers takes no responsibility for any damages, losses, or liabilities that may arise from the use or misuse of the information, products, or services provided in this publication.

For permissions requests or inquiries regarding this publication, please contact:

BLUEROSE PUBLISHERS
www.BlueRoseONE.com
info@bluerosepublishers.com
+91 8882 898 898
+4407342408967

ISBN: 978-93-5819-600-9

Cover design: Muskan Sachdeva
Typesetting: Rohit

First Edition: September 2023

Grateful Acknowledgement in Shaping of
"I have Resolved Not to Stop"

1. My Children - Daughters - Divya and Surabhi and Son, Gagan
2. My Late Brothers and Sisters
3. My friends - PP Sircar, Prem Gera and many more
4. My co-author - Aditi Sethi - who helped in more than one way
5. Amb(Retd) Abdul Majid Padar, who gave me direction and inspiration to embark on this project
6. And many more who encouraged in more than one way to set the goal and achieve it
7. And Most Importantly All the Dignitaries who have given their encouraging Comments, at its Manuscript Stage.
8. With pardon to those, whom I may have inadvertently not mentioned.
9. Pradeep Gupta, my friend and co-traveller.
10. Lest I forget My Dear Nephew, Gorav Bajaj, who extended wholehearted help.

*Dedicated to loving parents who brought
me up and moulded me to what I am!*

- Rana Pratap Bajaj

I dedicate this venture to my late Father Sh. Pardeep Chawla for planting the seed of travel in my head early on and showering his blessing on me from the laps of heaven

– Aditi Sethi

Author's Note

Rana Pratap Bajaj

I was born on 30th November 1943 in the district of Jalandhar of Punjab at my maternal place. I hail from an ordinary but honest and disciplined family and being the eldest child in the family I naturally got more attention than the siblings. After graduation, I was lucky to have been selected to serve in the Foreign Service of India. This naturally gave me the opportunity to travel and live abroad for a major period of my service. I had 8 long stints in different countries and was also able to travel to nearly 40 other countries. The lure of travel never got quenched even after my retirement in 2003. After marriage of my youngest child, son, Gagan, we did spend some time together visiting our children in USA and even taking care of our grandchildren. Life was going on and it was in Feb 2013, my wife Tripta met with a tragic accident. Life was no longer the same and I was also reaching an advanced stage. Then after elapse of a couple years, I realized and resolved that I would not allow hibernation to set in and would make most of my remaining years on earth. So, the search of India extensively and intensively started, which gave me zeal not only to live on but enjoy as much as possible. So, I have ventured into an attempt to share my experiences with my readers, not as a scholar but as a commoner would like to do. Without feeling a miss but enjoy to the core every moment as it comes, naturally. This philosophy will benefit many, only if it is developed. Not at all a difficult task and reap immense benefits and enrich yourself.

Rana Pratap Bajaj
June 2023

Aditi Sethi

Born in a small town of Sonipat, Haryana in 1985 to middle class but well-educated family. My parents ensured that both their kids, me being the younger one, got the best education despite the fact that we lived in a small city. Post completing my B.Tech followed by MBA from the best institutes of India, I had the opportunity to embark upon my quest to travel to new lands within India and even Internationally. Travel was a natural liking, perhaps It is the trait I have inherited from my father. The process of co-authoring this book with Mr. Rana P. Bajaj has been a fulfilling experience for me and my pursuit to travel to new lands and explore new things.

Thank you, Mom, Kapil and Advik, for your never-ending support. This would not have been possible without you all.

Prologue

When I turned 73, momentarily it flashed in my mind, that perhaps time is ripe to enter into Sanyas Ashram, as per old tradition and that I should go for seclusion in some cave or hill. But then, I thought and rightly so that I have successfully discharged my duties as Parent but have had hardly any time for 'Total Self'. It is not that I never had time to enjoy in the past, yet it somehow never fulfilled desire for that missing exclusiveness. It is true that by that time, my knees had almost given up but not my spirits, which were still high, and my mind was still active and agile.

Hence, **I RESOLVED NOT TO STOP** but 'Go On' exploring those parts of the world, which had, so far, remained uncovered. It is true that I first thought of exploring those parts of India, which had remained somehow uncovered. No one will disagree with me that there are many facets of India. Adventure is aplenty and spread all around. How can I then neglect such an opportunity, so embarked on my travels to various parts of India. Who would not like to have glimpses of my explorations and get encouraged to rekindle their spirits! Lest one misses God given opportunity, hopefully, my advice will get translated into reality and only then one will realize that instead regretting over having missed opportunities, it is much better to grab them.

Every nook and corner of the world has so much to give us that there should be no time to slacken. I have not stopped at turning 80, so how could you! So, get encouragement to pack up your bags and become Modern Day's Don Quixote!

Rana Pratap Bajaj

Contents

1. Exploring God's Own Country – Kerala at 73..................1
2. Invigorating, Multi-dimensional Sikkim at 74 19
3. Ladakh - Not merely Land of Lamas at 75....................37
4. In the lap of Dhauladhar, Palampur at 76 65
5. Dev Bhumi, Himachal Pradesh at 76..........................75
6. Revisit of Ladakh and Kayakalp at 76......................101
7. Gujarat Visit at 78.......................................127
8. Recalling Lake City Nainital 153
9. Uttarakhand - Holy and Wholesome at 78 157

Epilogue..179

Navarasa Kathakali Centre, Kerala

1st chapter

Exploring God's Own Country — Kerala at 73

Exploring God's Own Country – Kerala at 73 - Year 2016
Kerala - The Spice Land, not merely literally but also in reality

During 40-year of my career with the Government of India, I was privileged to travel to most parts of the world, having served in eight countries for a period of three to four years each and also having covered another 30-odd countries, on short spells. In India also I had travelled to some places, but I had not gone to Kerala - God's Own Country though I have always been enchanted by its sheer name, Kerala, and having read and heard from colleagues about Kerala's natural beauty and as it has much to offer, by way of traditional massage, seafood, spices, tea, wildlife, etc. Hence, I was looking for an opportunity to go to Kerala and had made enquiries from a couple of places. Having used to pampered travel and hotel stay, I looked for comfort on any journey. What I was looking for was being really taken care of during my visit or not. I am alone and without companion, and on top of that I have some physical difficulty in walking and some psychological barriers to strain myself physically. Therefore, naturally, I was looking for some assistance during journey and stay in Kerala. It was then that I came across a post in my Facebook page of Senior World. The package looked attractive for it was offering exactly what I was looking for. I contacted Nishant Chaudhury of Senior World. He not only promised but paid a visit to my residence to explain the whole plan. It fit my will and bill. I paid 50% and booked for the November 2016 trip. I did not look for other options and preferred to patronize them to give it a try. From service industry, especially travel, one wants comfort, if not luxury. Possibly, someone might have been able to match or even offer better services than the Senior World, I preferred to stick with them to find out for myself whether whatever was being sold by them is actually translated into practice or not. I got proper information and on given date went to their office for a get-together with fellow travellers. Only half of them had turned up but the co-travellers appeared friendly and were indeed looking forward for the trip.

Fishermen Boat in a Village of Kochi where Chinese Fishing Nets are found.

As was planned, we assembled in Terminal 3 of IGI airport on November 13 of 2016, where for the first time, I met Deepu and of course Nishant of Senior World. On halfway to the airport, I realized that I had left my phone at home and was in a dilemma what to do. I had decided to buy another phone for trip use but when I told Deepu, I was assured that it should pose no difficulty for he will arrange regular information about me and my trip to my daughter and I will be able to make calls from his phone as and when I require. Additionally, the co-travellers also offered to help me in this regard. Some familiarisations with co-travellers had started. The baggage and check-in were taken care by Senior World Team, and we proceeded towards the given gate number to board Vistara's flight to Goa via Mumbai and onwards to Kochi.

After a pleasant journey, we reached Kochi. The crew was helpful, and the service was pleasant. A few days ago, order of demonetization of high value notes had come, I was able to muster limited cash and was a little apprehensive whether I would be able to manage or not. Yes, of course, I had my Debit Card but was not sure whether it would be acceptable or not. However, during the entire journey, this factor did not pose a single problem and everything went smoothly. Firstly, there was hardly any extra expenditure and whatever if at all there was, my purse had sufficient to carry on. Additionally, the debit card made me really rich, as it was accepted almost at every place. I may also share here that unlike in the North, in Kerala people showed no undue haste and would not waste time queuing up. Knowing well that banks generally open at 1000 hrs, people will place their pass books only in advance in an orderly manner and would start assembling only at around 1000 hrs and not like in the North from 0400 hrs in the morning or even overnight. Patience did pay off and there were no unnecessary clamours. Debit Card acceptance made things even easier. Limited acceptance of old notes for full value was also seen as the shopkeepers really wanted to assist and had no craving to fleece. Also, the number of banks and ATMs was much more than here. Perhaps, the small population and self-ordained discipline also paid the dividends. Others will be well advised to take some lessons from this.

Now, let me proceed with the journey further, as it too had interesting instances and memorable moments. In Kochi, all 25 (including the 2 coordinators of Senior World) sat in a comfortable deluxe bus, which had additionally a guide and a PA system. Cold water bottles were given to quench the thirst and the guide started giving narration of various high points in route, like he pointed to back water, port area, beaches, roads leading to other places. Coconut trees were in abundance. It took a little over than an hour to reach the hotel. Welcome drinks were served, the check-in was taken care of and in the meantime briefing of the programme for the remaining day was given. In this while, I used Deepu's courtesy to inform my daughter about my safe arrival in Kochi. She, however, confirmed that she had been getting periodical feedbacks about our journey. Rooms were

I have Resolved NOT to Stop

comfortable, and after a wash and hot tea, we assembled in the lobby for visit to Chottanikkara Temple, for which we were briefed to be better attired in Longi, as in the temple vests/shirts/belts were not allowed. The Darshans were done in an orderly manner and everyone queued up. The devotion and reverence were visible. The evening prayers were being offered. Drumbeats and bells were making melodious sounds. Sandal pastes and lotus flowers were being offered to the deity and duly blessed bundle of these were given back. No commotion and only devotion was visible. Prasadam one could buy. The temple also had a lot many people sitting all around and perhaps they were alms seekers during day. We felt blessed and started on way back for dinner and in the bus, we were briefed about the next day's programme, which briefly was to assemble in the lobby after breakfast around 0830. I slept like a log, feeling tired after almost a day long travel but my mind was relaxed after my temple visit and satisfying dinner.

As the following day was going to be an eventful one, I wanted to take a real rest and feel fresh when I woke up. Exactly, this happened and I felt lily fresh the following morning and finishing my daily chores after bed tea, I was ready to start my second day of the trip, which had so far gone as I was looking for. As advised, baggage was kept outside the room for collection and taken to the bus for the onward journey. Like dinner, the breakfast too had a good mix spread of vegetarian and non-vegetarian dishes from the South and North of India and being plentiful providing more than ordinarily needed calories. On assembly, we started with Hi-Hi, Ha-Ha sessions. These were indeed Camera-Click sessions for the group. Where Deepu, who mainly served as the main photographer would call out 'Hi-Hi' to be responded by us with 'Ha-Ha' thus making being snapped an experience while getting the right focus and click. After initiation into 'Hi-Hi, Ha, Ha!' we alighted the bus for morning sight-seeing or rather a guided tour with local guide on board. Plenty of cold bottled water was available, which Nishant would dutifully give to everyone as also make sure that our headcount was complete.

The tour-day started with our first halt at the Dutch Palace. The local guide was well versed with history of the places and explained to us in detail that it was actually built by the Portuguese and given to the local

King to appease him. It was a two-Storey building. It was the first floor which had all the artefacts, paintings etc. Raja Ravi Varma's creations were excellent. Paintings on the walls were full of details of subjects from Hindu mythology. The robes kept there were spotless. It indeed presented a mirror of glimpses of the era these belonged to. Close-by there was a temple too. We were also joined by another co-passenger, by the name, Shree. He had worked in Saudi Arabia and could spell magic with his mathematical skills. Our next stop was the Jewish Synagogue built in 1568. It was well kept and spotlessly clean. It was the only Synagogue which witnesses regular service. It was not very far from the Dutch Palace and the area is known as Fort Cochin. It was decorated magnificently with blue tiles, which were hand painted and only a discerning eye would be able to notice that each tile was somewhat different than the others. There were Belgian chandeliers adorning the Synagogue. On the way one can find a number of shops carrying artefacts and antiques. Of course, one can also find other shops selling Kerala silk scarves, sarees, dresses, spices and fragrances. Some of us did buy a few items.

Thereafter, we went to see St Francis' Church, which was built in 1503 by Franciscan Friars and believed to be the oldest European Church. Vasco de Gama had landed in India in 1498 and within 5 years it was raised. The church also had the remains of Vasco de Gama's grave without, of course remains of his body, which was taken back by his son to Portugal. I recall, mention of this coming during our trip to Portugal in 1998. Renovation work was going on. The compound also had a Sandal tree. Though seemingly the Church appears small, if one were to see it from the perspective of the year of its erection, but counting the number of faith followers congregated at that time, it was really grand and definitely had a futuristic vision behind it. Close-by was our next target of the forenoon in the form of Chinese fishing nets. It was told to us that these were introduced by the traders from the Court of the Chinese Ruler, Kublai Khan. The nets were helpful in increasing catch of fish. The local fishermen have ever since adopted these nets reaping benefits. Fresh catch of various species of fish and other sea creatures, like lobsters, prawns, crabs, one could see displayed for sale by fishermen. We, however, settled for fresh coconut water feeling

I have Resolved NOT to Stop

warm and thirsty and felt refreshed thereafter. Before bidding goodbye, the local guide took us to a nice restaurant for those caring for lunch before embarking on more than 4-hour bus ride to witness much talked about scenic beauty of Munnar, our next destination and night halt.

Nilgiri's Tahar - Mountain Goat in Ernakulam National Park

Munnar is a famous hill station and supposedly the heart of Kerala. After lunch, we started on our first drive of the day. For a while, it was plains and before starting for journey to hills, we stopped at a way-side cafeteria and enjoyed one of the best hot masala teas. Both aroma and taste were really refreshing. On the way we had seen rubber being tapped. After having been refreshed by tea, now it was fun time. The journey time was well utilized in introducing ourselves on PA system in the bus and the rest of the time was used in playing Tambola, where again Deepu became the Master of Ceremonies and lo! I was lucky to win prizes for full houses twice besides other side prizes. The time was spent so fruitfully and with a lot of fun, that the ordeal of the journey was never felt and in fact a bond developed with co-passengers. Some traits of the co-passengers came to be known. Surprisingly, Deepu proved to be an entertainer and a good singer. Rays, Mrs. Vishwanath - Doctor of Music, Ashok - running PG Hostel, Mrs. Ganguli, Kataria were good singers too. Col Ganguli was practicing Medical Doctor; Anjana Jacob had been a banker. Mr. Ray had worked for Nestle. Mr. Gupta had worked for Delhi Government. Vishwanathan a good Cricketer. Rays had a love marriage; Bengali boy having met his soulmate in a Sikh girl. There were builders, architect, etc. Mrs. Meenu, whose daughter happened to be with Ethiopian Embassy in Delhi was also there. Of course, everyone was out to enjoy and have a merry time. Touch wood! everyone was caring and sharing. What more to expect!

As the destined hotel was perched on a hill, we were carried to the hotel on jeeps. There was a narrow bridge, and the distance was just about 1 Km but it cannot be navigated by bus. Welcome drink, check-in was completed in a jiffy. After freshening up, I was joined by Shree. He proved to be an excellent roommate and a good companion. We both enjoyed our evening drinks and thereafter went to have a well-spread dinner. After a fitful sleep, I awoke next day around 6 am. We had our morning tea and settled to finish morning calls so as to be ready, after breakfast for exploring Munnar, in reality. The hotel in which we had stayed in Munnar belonged to the same Omani Sheikh whose hotel in Abad we had stayed in Kochi. The hotel presented a class for selection of location, scenic beauty, running stream, flowers, furniture and furnishing, and well-behaved friendly staff. In brief comfort was assured and enjoyed. Naturally, breakfast, not lacking in any respect, made us fit to commence our day. Again, 1 Km journey across the bridge close to the main road was by jeeps while the bus waited for us to be picked up. There was indeed a well-coordinated drill from the point of view of comfort and assembling all the passengers. A little later, we were joined by a local guide, Rosy, who was originally from Tamil Nadu but had spent time in Kolkata and was training herself to be a professional guide. In the meantime, we got tempted to attempt home-made chocolates, signs of which were displayed just across the road. Believe me, we would have missed something if we had not tried nuts and raisins filled chocolates, fresh and tasty. We took express coach, as there was long que, to go to Ernakulam National Park to see rare Nilgiris Tahr - a Mountain goat and the Museum there. What a scenic beauty! It was spread for miles and covered by well-maintained tea plantations. In itself it was worth the entire visit. So soothing was the greenery and oxygen pumping in our lungs or rather cleansing our polluted lungs! Tahr was obliged to be snapped. On the way back after a short pedestrian trail, from where Tahr could be seen, and where one reaches to take a bus for backward journey, there was a small museum, describing about mountains, species of flora and fauna. People of a local tribe work on those mountains and generally do not mix with the general public, maintaining their tribal culture and customs. At that time tea and cold drinks were available from the local stall. The Way back journey again was very pleasant.

Outside Hotel Abad at Munnar with Deepu

It was time for a visit to the Tea Museum and we could see the process of tea making of different kinds. The plantation shop was selling different varieties of tea and explaining which one was best to acquire the real aroma. A percolator type device was also available. We purposely skipped the film show on tea processing. Most of us bought different varieties of tea. I gathered that the factory and plantation were owned by Tatas and in fact nearly 90% of the tea plantation was owned by Tatas. For workers, there were houses with caring facilities, like sanitation, water and electricity. It was time for lunch in a local restaurant. The Thali system was much in vogue but A La Carta arrangements were also there. Experience has shown that

Thali works out better, as ordered by most of us. This ensures consumption of cooked food and daily fresh preparations. I also tried Kerala rice, thick but tasty and goes well with Sambhar and Rasam. Now eyes were looking for something new and marvellous spots.

Waiting Anxiously for Paraiyar Lake Adventure

Our next destination was about an hour's scenic drive to Mattupetty Dam. It cannot be compared with Bhakra Dam but the scenic beauty visible for miles was another matter. Filled with the charm of natural beauty and giving a real treat to the eyes besides soothing fresh air for the mind, made us hesitant to march on return journey. Tea plantations, bamboo and other trees were in abundance. We could also spot an elephant, though we were told at times, there comes a herd. On return to the hotel, we were told to assemble in a lounge after about an hour and a half. We made a wild guess that there must be something cooking up in Deepu's mind. Yes, it was so, as on arrival in the designated Lounge, we learnt it was birthday of Meenu. However, before the cake cutting ceremony, we played a Guessing Game. In this,3 the entire group was divided in two equal parts and each one of us was given a slip and pencil to write down some peculiarity about oneself, which in general may not be known to the group. The coordinators distributed the slips. I was able to recognize the 'Badminton Champion'. Mrs. Anjana Jacob, however, she could not pick me up correctly, as I had scribbled 'mischievous' for myself and all along she thought me to be a simpleton and thus did not even dare to ask me. It was great fun. (Incidentally, on a later NE trip again, I could not be identified, as I had written ' Man for All Seasons' as my trait.) With proper candlelight, the cake cutting ceremony was done. Songs were sung by many, and Nishant gave a very good dance number and was joined by other group members. Sree came out with his mathematical magical tricks and made people spellbound. On the whole, the fun was unlimited and made us forget the tiredness of the day. However, some of us, as usual were struck by their style of combating tiredness. I had seen Tapioca plants on the way and was wondering whether these were made some use of or not. In Tanzania, it was called Casava and serves as staple diet. Charcoal-Roasted Casava was available on the roadside there. Deepu brought Banana chips, which I knew are plenty in Kerala, but he also brought Casava Chips, which are crisper than even banana chips. Perhaps, moist climate of Kerala is not that suitable for Potato chips as Banana and Casava chips. Freshly crackled and grounded spices were being used by the hotel kitchen, making food more aromatic. The dinner was again a treat and especially roasted fish in banana leaf was very tasty. Some of us tried traditional Kerala massage in hotel before dinner. We retired to our rooms for n sound nigh sleep, as the next morning we were to assemble again after breakfast and leaving our packed baggage outside our rooms for onward journey to Thekkady.

Glimpses of the Birthday Celebration at Munnar Hotel

After getting ready for the day, I could not believe that three days had already passed. Busy time in enjoyment had not left any clue that it was the 4th day. Healthy breakfast assured us that we were fit for the 4-hour drive to Thekkady. Hi-Hi, Ha-Ha session was repeated, and, in the meantime, our bags were placed in jeeps for further journey. We switched on to bus and Nishant after his drill of having head count, gave signal for go-ahead. Watching scenic beauty of Munnar, once again we were taking a long drive on circuitous hilly roads. For spending time, we took shelter of Antakshri and believe me, how time passed enjoyably, I can hardly explain. There were teams, yet no teams and the idea was just to have fun. Songs after songs, some old, some new and also songs with which some memories of us were associated were sung. Baritone voice of some made the melodies even sweeter. On way we stopped for some beverages and some of us bought bottles of herbal oil for our own use and gift. On reaching Thekkady, we entered a restaurant for lunch. The place was typical Malabari. The food was fresh, hot and reasonably priced. We then arrived at the hotel and were served a welcome drink and retired to our assigned rooms and after washing re-assembled in the lobby. The hotel again was of the Abad Group and instead of on a plain plot, its living rooms were on a sloppy hill, with well-maintained garden, full of flowers, which made the view more scenic and after sunset the lights added to it even more charm. The architecture of the lobby also gave a feeling of welcome, as it was spacious and open with comfortable sitting arrangements.

The bus took us to Paraiyar Sanctury. The sanctuary has a lot of monkeys and is quite used to human folks. We took boat ride to Paraiyar Lake. We were accommodated in 3 boats for one and half hour ride, with proper lifeguards. On shore one could see various animals grazing. We could identify mainly elephants, bison, antelopes, monkeys and sambhar. I wish we could have had binoculars, as it would have helped us to see wildlife more clearly. In water crocodiles and otters, one could notice. There were also many types of birds. It was enjoyable as the boats sailed smoothly and virtually glided on the water. On our return to hotel, we enjoyed our evening tea and re-assembled for a Kathakali performance nearby. Our seats were reserved in the front. The show started on time. The artists were in their large, colourful costumes and elaborate makeup. Without speaking a word, hand gestures, thumping feet and facial movements were used to narrate the story, taken from Hindu mythology. The artists were definitely adept and their facial expressions, mainly their eyes were doing the talking. To add comic twist, the artist who was performing the role of a lady, called the most eligible looking bachelor of the group, Nishant on the stage. Through gestures, Nishant was made to admit that he likes her. She then demanded a gold chain (Mangla Sutra) for her. Nishant was in a dilemma and on refusal was pushed to a side hut to exit. It was hilarious and got good applause from the audience. Thereafter, some of us got photographed with the artists. The show ended. Some of us wanted to also see Kalarippayattu - an ancient form of martial art from Kerala. However, unfortunately, that day the show was fully booked. It was left for another time. Some went for body massages and shopping. I was told that spices be bought best in Alleppey, our next destination.

Group Picture before departure from Thekkady for Allepey

Of course, late evening was open for sundowners, after enjoying which we had our dinner, which was well laid out as expected. The hotel is divided in three main sections: the living area, the lobby and the dining area. All separate but passing through a well adorned garden, thus giving a look of vastness of the property, displaying richness as against stinginess to save small spaces to accommodate one thing or the other. Duly briefed for the next morning to be ready for assembly after breakfast, we left for our respective rooms. Pleasant, nice sleep made us to awake fresh and relaxed. After finishing our daily routine and packing our baggage, we were ready for another eventful day.

Glimpse of Spice Garden

On 5th day, the 17th November, we assembled in the lobby after breakfast and before saying goodbye we had our group snaps taken. It was a 4-hour scenic journey to Alleppey. Time in the bus was spent cracking jokes, singing songs, listening to music and lo! we reached Spice Garden, close to Allepey. We were taken around the spice garden and explained, as to how spices were collected, from Cardamom (black and green), cloves, nutmeg, cinnamon, black pepper, etc. The most interesting was Green Cardamom, which grows on cane like sticky plants, close to roots, akin to sugarcane seeds. Of course, I knew this having seen for myself, in another spice island, Zanzibar, which incidentally, took spice plantation from Kerala by Arab traders. Omani King was then the ruler of Zanzibar. Zanzibar happens to be the setting of stories of Arabian Nights and now forms part of Tanzania (with mainland Tanganyika). The spices were definitely fresh. We were explained that good quality black pepper is small in size and cloves when plucked must ooze oil, otherwise cloves are not fresh. There was hardly any difference in prices but definitely the quality and freshness, which matters a lot for freshness of any spice is its soul and were definitely par excellence. The place also had herbal soaps, oils, medicaments and other products. We did carry these for their worth and being produced by the source, guaranteeing satisfaction. Our bus took us to a village on the shores of Lake Vembanad. It was no longer check-in, in any hotel but turn to enjoy a night stay in Kettuuvallam, the luxurious deluxe air-conditioned houseboat. After crossing a couple of house boats, we reached houseboat marked for us, which was one of the three in which the group was accommodated. Beer was there to quench thirst and serve as appetizer, before devouring freshly cooked lunch, on the cruising boat. In clicking, chatting, sipping beer time passed and after meal, the boat ride on the lake made many of our dreams fulfilled.

Ladies get tempted to pluck within reach fresh coconuts at the traditional village on the shores of Lake Vemabanad

Past 5.30 in the evening, the boat anchored near a village. The facility of traditional massage was available, which I also availed of. In the meantime, Deepu picked fresh King Prawns and fish for the dinner. Both were sweet and tender. After the massage was done, I got a herbal bath and came on the boat. After change over, it was about time to think of evening drink. On another boat, Meenu showed her culinary skills. Songs, music and snapping made the time to slip away unnoticed and again freshly cooked dinner made the evening divine. Sea breeze and a little rocking boat made the night sleep relaxing.

Kethuuvallam, the Luxurious Deluxe Air-conditioned Houseboat at the Lake Vemabanad

About sunrise the next morning we awoke. Deepu and Nishant got busy clicking and capturing the best and we got a visual treat for our eyes. After finishing morning chores and a satisfying breakfast, on day 6, November 18, we started our journey back to the village. Birds, coconut trees and morning light on the shores presented an unforgettable spectacle. In village small Kerala bananas and coconut water we could enjoy and alighted bus for return to Kochi. On way we stopped at Marari Beach in Kochi. The white sand beach is one of the best in Kerala. Again, some of us chose to at least wet our feet. Everyone enjoyed moments in their own way and got clicked. In Kochi, we had our lunch. Again, the food was freshly cooked and served with butter milk and Rasam, both enjoyably tasty. Some of us thereafter went to one of the famous departmental stores to buy silks. Shree bid good-bye there. On way to airport, we stopped at one place to buy freshly prepared chips of banana and casava; coconut oil and we also tasted Kerala Halwa, which was then being made, oven-fresh or cauldron fresh.

Being a group of 25, the airline, allowed priority checking and ensured an on time departure. After enjoying hospitality of airline, reached Delhi airport around 10 PM. The Senior World Coordinators collected baggage and handed over to us. It was time to say good-bye, with promise to be in touch and if possible, meet again, preferably, on another trip. Telephone numbers were already exchanged, and we continue to exchange greetings, messages and seeking welfare and thus creating a bond. Life becomes easier, when one has someone to seek welfare and more so when you look forward for a reunion. It was a God given opportunity in his own country and was facilitated by Senior World. To the extent of being accused of eulogizing Senior World, I would not deter from patting them for performance and would be the last to hesitate to try them again. In fact, one of my known persons, Sadhna Jain was encouraged after seeing my album, provided by Senior World to undertake a Sri Lanka trip and indeed thanked me for a wonderful experience. God willing, I shall be on one of their next trips. My advice to them would be to add, a few more destinations, like Madhya Pradesh and Gujarat.

It is not the end of my pursuit for travel and wandering, as sooner than later, I should be on another trip and needless to add, that I do promise to share with you Moments of Joy, so that you too do not lag behind and take benefit of my tips, which I am confident will make your journey really awesome!

I have Resolved NOT to Stop

Natu La Pass Visit Certification

2nd chapter

Invigorating, Multi-dimensional Sikkim at 74

Sikkim and Darjeeling - with a peeping View of Mount Kangchenjunga

My readers must have felt positive vibes while going through the journey of Kerala. I can therefore be certain that what is going to be uncovered now, will be even more interesting. If in Kerala there was back-water from the sea, in the coming pages you will find tantalizing places. So, please keep with me, and I assure that what is going to unfold will be even more worth grasping or should I say emulating because you will be roaming where there are superb spectacles, simple and smiling people, organic food and pollution free fresh air even though thin at places like Nathu La, yet invigorating and life-time experience!

Once again, I opted for the services of Senior World. Their coordinators travelled with the group of 20+ ensuring personal care foreach one of the travellers, right from assembly point at the airport. Naturally, travelling becomes hassle-free and we could concentrate on enjoying the journey for the purpose meant for. Further, the hotels selected by them were comfortable; the food was always good in all respects, including varieties and travel to places of interest was always convenient. Of course, there was pre-travel get-together to acquaint with each other and to equip ourselves as per requirements of the travel and places involved.

Precisely, it was on Sunday, the 16th April 2017 that 24 of us (including 2 Coordinators) started from Delhi airport by Southern

Airlines flight to Bagdogra (WB) and sat tension free in flight after having handed over our bags and getting preferential seating, Wheelchairs for those, like me, who needed them were available. On arrival at Bagdogra, groups of 4-5 persons each were made and each group was assigned individual Innova vehicles and we started our onward journey to Darjeeling and in the meantime the coordinators ensured that the baggage of each one of us was put on individually assigned cars. Bagdogra is a big Cantonment Area and one can see tea plantations immediately after the commencement of journey. Having had lunch on flight each one of us was comfortable to proceed. For quenching thirst cool bottled water was available. Watching the scenic beauty of tea plantations and trees, mostly Teak, we proceeded on a circuitous path. The roads were really rough, but the experienced drivers made the journey as comfortable as was possible. After a short journey, the hill climb had started. On way to Darjeeling, we saw other varieties of trees, like Pine. We stopped on our way to have refreshing tea and stretch our legs.

There is an advantage to starting to travel for sight-seeing earlier. One remains fit and can enjoy the most, otherwise lethargy sets in. Of course, it also depends on person to person. Well, I must admit, that I am a bit lazy and therefore miss some fun, but on the whole, I enjoy it immensely. Group travel has advantages as it takes care of a lot of things. One enjoys the company of co-travellers, gets entertained by various skills of theirs, and above all there is a feeling of security. Sharing of lifetime experiences, learning from others, and being taken care of and extending a helping hand to your companions and of course, developing better understanding with one's life-partner, if one is lucky to be so accompanied. In our group, the senior most was 82 years and admittedly more fit than I felt myself. The Easy life spent earlier was showing clear disadvantage. Active life would have given me more opportunities to watch closely although I was not left out, yet I felt lagging behind. Nevertheless, it gave me a lot of encouragement to strive and match the rest even though partly.

In the car we travelled in, were 5 persons (other than the driver). All with different backgrounds, but all out to have fun and enjoy themselves. We shared our life-time experiences both are personal and professional while traveling. It was good past time and learning from each other. There were Col (Retd) Kanwal Deep Singh and his wife Daljeet Kaur. Both extremely nice persons and a great company. Made for each other couple. Daljeet alias Guddi was a great singer and liked modelling at each given opportunity. Whenever time arose, she did try to put on local attire and gave great poses. She could recall songs during the Antakshri Sessions and win single-handedly. Even now, both of them are in touch with me.

The other couple was Rupinder Kaur and JS Kathuria. Kathuria was a banker. A gentlemen and a great host. We liked and enjoyed each other's company. Though, Col. Kanwal Deep Singh had served in NE (Shillong), he particularly wanted to visit Sikkim and likewise Kathurias Who had served in Kolkata were keen to re-visit NE. The lure of mountains and a pollution free atmosphere have their own charm. One is able to see from close angles, the rich cultures, customs and enjoy cuisines, meet people and understand the heritage better. Achievements of different parts and the advantages or disadvantages of different places, one is able to witness personally. It is always to learn.

As I have said earlier, group travel has advantages, but further advantages come from travelling with an organized group. I could see the difference. One is taken care of totally. Even one has not to worry about clicking , the organizers did this for us and kept informed our family members back home our daily progress during journey. No spectacle was missed and having keen eye for photography, the scenes were better chosen, selected and clicked. Photographs were posted on net and even each one of us was given an album to serve as a life-time memoir. Incidentally, in any unfortunate circumstances, like someone falling ill on way, extended hand of help of the organizers comes in handy, e.g. during that very journey, Col. Ravinder Bhat got indisposed and when local medical help proved insufficient, the family was brought back to Delhi for proper and timely medical help. He recovered and was extremely thankful. In group one is also able to meet people who have retired after successful careers in service, Services, business, and professions. One may get encouraged when someone from the

I have Resolved NOT to Stop

Group tells you that she has been single for 22 years and brought up her family striving alone. Living example!

I must now proceed with the onward journey of the first day, after having had crunchies and munchies brought by some families and savoured with refreshing Darjeeling tea! Enjoying flora and fauna on the way to Darjeeling, after a three-hour car journey we reached our hotel which was comfortable and conveniently located. I retired to my room and met the co-occupant of the room, Pardeep Kumar Gupta, who had retired from the Forest Service of Himachal Pradesh and only last December had lost his wife, who had retired as Principal of a College in Chandigarh and had suffered from brain cancer. What a co-incidence that I too lost my wife on 23rd February 2013 in a tragic road accident, after she bravely fought back and survived breast-cancer after having head surgery and radiation therapy. Pardeep proved to be a good roommate and companion. We enjoyed whatever spare time we got together and spent it happily. We enjoyed our pre-dinner drinks, discussions and exchanging notes and on one spare afternoon we explored exclusively local cuisines. We found, among other things, local brew and Desi Chicken, with a wonderful and enjoyable taste that reminded him of Himachal and of course, I recalled my days in Myanmar. We have become life-long family friends. Breakfasts and Dinners were organized by the organizers in the hotels where they stayed. Sumptuous meals, nutritious and tasty for almost all pallets. Plenty and pleasant can sum-up meals. Lunches one was free to choose, either outside or in hotel, on payment basis. One had the option to skip, which I even though being a glut had opted to skip, having become overweight, still at times only and not always for food was so tempting that I did not care for bulging belly. That evening, after a day travell, we enjoyed dinner and retired to our rooms. Hotels provide a tea-coffee kettle in the room itself and therefore, one has not to worry about morning bed tea or evening tea of which one may have become habitual to, like I have.

After a sound sleep in a Darjeeling hotel, close to Gymkhana, I got up at 3 am to witness Sunrise Spectacle at Tiger Hill. It is not an event to be missed. The sunrays on Kanchenjunga fall, making it a, golden colour. Not less than 5000 persons had assembled, and local ladies were selling hot coffee to keep themselves warm, as it was chilly early morning. Other goodies, like selfie-rods, hand gloves, and caps were also being sold. Majestically the sun arose and all of us cheered up. It was a great feeling to have attained the objective, like Nirvana. A few of us missed it as it was optional and perhaps got deterred by the ordeal of early rising and perhaps later regretted having missed something which eyes can only capture, and memories can only retain and in no way, photographs narrate the whole story of the spectacle. It is comparable to witnessing a match in a stadium and being part of it among a roaring crowd rather than watching it on TV

Rising Sun Kangchenjunga View from Tiger Hill

I have Resolved NOT to Stop

Slowly, the march back started, as traffic was moving at a snail's pace. We were lucky to reach a Japanese temple and Pagoda, peaceful and serene monuments, clean and dignified. Drumbeats in the Japanese temple after a few moments of silence created a soulful sound and a craving reverence for the Almighty! It was naturally time to rush back to the hotel for freshening up and breakfast. Definitely, a soulful breakfast made me go full steam the whole day. Talking about "Steam" I shall revert back later-on. That day we visited 5 more points covering The Himalayan Mountaineering Institute, PNZ Zoological Park, Tenzing Rock, the Tibetan Self Help Refugee Centre and a tea garden, making one each for the original 7 sisters, as the NE was earlier known. All had distinct features and historical value. The Refugee Centre had collections of old photographs and typical artefacts, dresses, etc to sell. Unique and not exorbitantly priced, they made good items both for collection and as gift to friends and relations. Darjeeling Tea at the Tea Garden had limited variety but in the City there were aplenty of them. Out of curiosity I checked about ladies, who pluck tea leaves and I gathered, they are able to pluck from 7 to 12 Kgs of tea-leaves in a day and are paid anywhere from Rs. 10 to Rs. 15 per Kg. The finest quality of tea (mainly buds only) for aroma and used for blending costs a few thousand Rupees per Kg. There are several varieties of tea and one can spend days to learn about them. Here, at least a little knowledge was not found to be dangerous. Something got added to our knowledge, and the lush green site of the tea garden made our day.

Group at Lhamahatta Complex

In the afternoon, after lunch (optional), one could go for shopping close-by or enjoy a ride on the Toy Train (optional). I preferred and opted for the second. It is the highest rail track and runs both on 'Steam Engine' and Diesel Engine. The steam engine trip is priced high. The rails pass through the city on both sides of the road, crisscrossing and taking one on a memorable trip. It is a historical train, and one can remember many a song, 'Mere Sapon ki Rani...' 'Khoya Khoya Chand...' and so on, like 'Sau Sal Pahle'. One can reminisce about childhood days when one used to travel on trains run by Steam Engines, but it is now available only at a few places. One finds it amazing, that a narrow-gauge steam engine train still runs and carries on the heritage of Himalayas. On way of 2-hour journey, it makes stops (to and fro) to take water; halts at one scenic place, and goes up to Ghoom, where there is a small Rail Museum. The engine is kept running by taking good care in maintenance and checking various parts. The 'chukh-chukh' and 'steam whistle' make one say, 'Koi Lauta De Mere Bite Hue Din'. Of course, the Railways can add charm by serving Darjeeling Tea on trains to make the journey even more memorable and a life-time experience. Anyhow, it would be a pity if it were to be closed down, as it was being whispered.

The famous toy train in Darjeeling

Before I commence my journey on Day three from Darjeeling, it would be appropriate for me to tell some important things about Darjeeling itself. It is a city full of traffic jams, as almost half the roads are blocked by outside vehicles coming daily to bring passengers and carrying them back only in the evening. Therefore, it is advisable to start for any destination giving margin for heavy traffic, e.g. the Steam Engine train starts on dot as scheduled and there remains every chance to miss the trip by starting with lesser time. Also. there is variation in day and night temperatures. While it can be hot during daytime, evenings are cool. Also, one should ensure that the hotel booked in Darjeeling has enough parking place or arrangement as otherwise one may have to wait for one's vehicle or walk to get one. It is also important to keep in mind that while generally the highways are well maintained, the other roads need much more attention and therefore journey times are longer than one would normally estimate from the distance to the destination. Darjeeling is also known for good education for which there are various institutions

Our next destination was Namchi, Sikkim. It is the birthplace of the then incumbent CM of Sikkim (Pawan Chamling) and he has been nurturing that place with his heart and soul. On reaching Namchi that evening, when my son-in-law, Pawan asked me as to how I was, in my usual jocular response, I responded that I was in his fiefdom (namesake). The road up to Malli (border of WB with Sikkim) though full of turns, ups and downs is very good but after crossing the River Tista from the Sikkim border up to Namchi is patchy and full of ditches besides being narrow. One could notice the changing landscape. Roadside morning glory and other flowers made one's day. A Fresh breeze was also invigorating and made one almost forget about the tedious journey. My inquisitiveness about seeing flags of various colors flying near the roadside was quenched by our driver when he told us that the flags were Prayer Flags and had hymns appear in scripted form on them. Waving flags had their charm to attract our attention, welcoming and spreading a kind of peace. We also learnt that some flags are white, which represents the departed souls of dear ones. On the way we could also find orchards and farms (organic) for which Sikkim is known.

On reaching Namchi, one could see for oneself that it was a neat and clean city. On Mall one could find people relaxing and enjoying. Cheerfulness was visible. Also visible was the welcome given in traditional way by pleasing hotel staff. They applied Tilaks on our foreheads and covered us with ochre colour silk scarves. Soon after reaching our assigned rooms, the baggage arrived. It was handled in a systematic manner by Senior World Coordinators, who ensured tagging each bag with customized sturdy name cards at the very commencement of the journey. Likewise, individuals were given specially designed caps giving a distinct identity to the group. That showed their keenness to ensure comfort and perfection.

Near the Sikkim border on the river Tista, one could see people rafting. At another place, I saw people enjoying hang gliding. Almost Honk free driving and such spectacles make one closer to nature.

After a little rest and tea refreshment, we were ready to explore Namchi. The credit must go to the incumbent CM of Sikkim, for conceptualizing and execution to perfection of two religious complexes. The first is Chardham at Solophok Hill and the second is Guru Padma Shambhava's huge statue at Samdruptse Hill. That day we concentrated on the Chardham. Replicas of the four Dhams, namely, Badrinath, Jagannath, Dwarka and Rameshwar in their distinct architecture were both impressive and imposing. In addition, there were replicas of 12 Jyotirlingas. There are 64 priests on the premises, who all were well educated and further trained in Sanskrit and scriptures at Varanasi, Vrindavan and Hardwar/Rishikesh. They perform rituals with religious fervor and full devotion. There is Daily Aarti in the evenings and Abhisheks at given times. We were duly invited to light Aarti Lamps. Lord Shiva is supposed to have incarnated as Kirateshwar in Indrakeel (now Sikkim). At the time of the inauguration of Chardham, which was constructed over a period of more than six years, was inaugurated after performance of proper Yajna by Shankaracharya Saraswati ji Maharaj with the help of his 84 disciples. Lord Shiva in sitting pose is impressive. The trident of Lord Shiva is supposedly 108 feet tall. One can see Four Dham complex from other hills miles away. The complex is kept immaculately clean. One can also see in the hall behind the main temple, on walls well carved depictions from the life story of Lord Shiva.

I have Resolved NOT to Stop

There is a belief that at the site of Chardham, there was an ancient symbol of Lord Shiva. It was worth a visit, not merely for religious purposes but also from the point of architectural beauty that Chardham represents.

Chardham of Solophok Hill, Namchi (South Sikkim)

After that, we returned to the Hotel, and having Dinner, the time came to celebrate the birthday of one of the co-travellers, Manju Bansal. The cake was cut and all of us wished the couple long lives. It was merriment for a purpose and definitely overwhelmed the Bansals. In our group, people had joined from as far away as Lucknow,

Invigorating, Multi-dimensional Sikkim at 74

Himachal, Dehradun and Chandigarh. The group enjoyed cohesiveness and complete understanding and concentrated on enjoying every moment.

Gangtok, the capital of Sikkim, was the destination on Day 4. After King's breakfast we were on our way to Gangtok but only after a short while, we stopped to see Guru Padmasambhava's 135' tall statue. So impressive and captivating that I could understand how Guru Padmasambhava was able to spread Buddhism here. Another attraction was Ropeway. A little more than 1 kilometres long, the ropeway presents an impressive view of Namchi Valley. At the end of the ropeway was a small but beautiful garden. One can walk around and have lungful of clean air. Road to Gangtok was not totally metaled though at many places repair work was visible as also new roads were coming up. Progress was visible, as one could see from the road from gate to the actual statue site.

Guru Padmasambhava's 135' tall statue.

On reaching Gangtok and retiring to the hotel-room, one was free to go shopping in the nearby mall. It is known as Mahatma Gandhi Square because of his statue. It was a well-kept place, clean and with comfortable seatings and tiled floor. One can spend hours peacefully enjoying local bars close by or Ice-cream Parlour. Sikkim Rum or Millet brew (served hot) one may be enjoyed. In the evening a get-together was arranged, wherein all of us introduced ourselves formally, giving background; generally, it is done on the very first opportunity, even during a long bus-ride. We also played games and came to know many facets of fellow travellers. Certain aspects of one's personality got revealed and gave all of us pleasant surprise. Some turned out to be excelling in sports, some in cooking, some in social service and someone else in business. Talents were discovered. The bond was not only established among all of us, but it also got firmer and closer. Life-long friendships got established at this new place with no-longer new people.

Before preparing for Day 5, the Day 4 was closed with an evening drink with a roommate and a well-laid dinner. The food was tasty and not at all spicy-hot and it was a combination of vegetarian and non-vegetarian dishes. The ingredients definitely showed freshness.

Day 5 started, with freshening up, followed by a well-spread breakfast. I especially enjoyed the pure honey and lemon drink, so refreshing and appetizing. One could choose from a wide variety of dishes from various parts of India. Unity in diversity was amply translated. Rid of hunger, made us embark on city tour. We enjoyed an educational visit to the Research Institute of Tibetology. It has a collection of coins, artifacts and scriptures from Tibet and even currency notes from the former Principality of Sikkim. Thereafter, we went to enjoy the ropeway. During journey on the ropeway, the atmosphere turned to merriment with instant spell of Antakashri. Soulful singing made the mood swinging. Though it was only for a short while, the joy lasted for hours. We went to have closer view of Kanchenjunga from Tashi Viewpoint. On a clear day, one is able to feel almost face to face with Kanchenjunga. At the bottom of Viewpoint, one can enjoy fresh pineapple and surprisingly Golgappas. How could we have lagged behind and we definitely indulged in devouring both. Thereafter, we went to Ganesh Talk (Temple), which is revered, and one enclosure also gives opportunity to get a circular view of entire valley. The priests perform special puja invoking Lord Ganesha's blessings with small offerings only and one feels blessed and elated.

Group Picture at Banjihakhri falls

That day's another high point of that day was a visit to the Banjihakhri Waterfalls. It is worshipped by local tribes. A Cool splash definitely makes one feel fresh. Some of us attired ourselves in local costumes (available on hire) and got ourselves snapped. Some braved to cross over the fall on a rope-bridge. Some even took holy water in bottles to bring back. Who can deny one's faith in any ritual or practice besides such places being spectacles to watch and enjoy view and preserve it for future! On returning hotel, one was free to shop and explore. I too collected a couple of things for gifting. Evening was again a merriment time with drinks and a lavish dinner. This ensured sound sleep. Luckily, it did not rain during the day but Gangtok nights did witness rains and consequently, a slight chill in the weather but not unbearable, was noticeable. We, of course, waited for the next day, as it was going to be the high point of our visit to Sikkim.

To have more fun on Day 5 itself, some of us chose to go to local Casino. God knows, whether it was to earn money or burn money, either way unlimited fun was guaranteed!

The organizers of the tour had well prepared themselves for Day 6, which I would call culmination day of our journey, by applying and obtaining necessary permits for those interested in going to Nathu La, important theatre of the 1962 Chinese Aggression. In the local language it is known as 'Pass of Listening Ears'. Its altitude is 14,100 feet and the air remains thin. Fog forms quickly. Therefore, there are strict visiting times. The permits are checked at several places and it was definitely chilly, but we had prepared ourselves carefully with heavy Woollens, gloves and cap. Some even carried masks, special boots and an ice stick as the last few meters climb are slippery and narrow. It is on Old Silk Road and travellers from China, like Huein Tsang and Fa Hein came through this pass in 5th and 6th century respectively. It is also on the official Kailash Manasarovar pilgrimage route. On a clear day one is able to see Chinese border posts and soldiers. The importance of the place gets enhanced, as it was the meeting place of border personnel from both sides. The Tibetan refugees came to India in 1959 through this pass, after Tibet was annexed by China. For us it was no less historical day. One can get a signed Certificate of having visited Nathu La for a small fee of Rs. 120/-; worth trim money! One must appreciate the Jawans posted and performing arduous duties there, My Salute and Jai Hind.

No less commendable is the work of the Border Road Organization, who have made and maintained in tough weather, facing landslides, metaled high-speed two-lane roads. For lunch, a way side eating joint served freshly prepared fried rice and tea, both wholly satisfying.

We then came to Baba Harbhajan Shrine, popularly known as Baba Mandir. Baba ji was a Jawan of the Army and had died while escorting a mule column on 4th October 1968. His body got carried 2 Kms away by a fast current. As per legend he appeared in the dreams of one of his colleagues informed him exact location of his body and belongings and suggested the construction of his 'Samadhi'. After body and belongings were found at the said place, the unit did construct a 'Samadhi', which in November 1982 was relocated 9 Kms from the original site at a more conveniently approachable place.

He is revered by Indian soldiers, who do not forget to pay a visit to Baba Mandir and carry with them blessed water from there to remove any trouble from their family members, by following certain rules for 21 days. Even Chinese troops are said to believe Baba ji appeared on white horse in white clothes. He has been accorded the status of Saint and Indian Army personnel see in him their protector. Indian Army also accorded one of the high medal and rank of Hony Major and accordingly to his given status, he gets treated.

At Natu La Post

It was now time to rush to see 50 feet deep oval shape Tsomgo Lake. The hills around were covered with snow. Many persons with decorated Yaks were waiting at the lake so that people like us could enjoy Yak Ride and have a Snap by paying a small amount of Rs. 50/-. They could manage to lift me up on Yak and I could get myself snapped peacefully. It gave me a real thrill, no chill. It was a wonderful experience worth every dime. The lake is home to Brahmini ducks and other migratory birds. The journey back was very slow, as thick fog had started appearing and after covering a few kilometres it was almost pitch dark. The drivers were adept at negotiating curves safely and matching them. Of course, they would stop at certain places. A little more rain had started and the fog started thinning out. We came safely to the hotel. Some of us again ventured to the Casino whereas we decided to call co-travellers interested in a joint evening drink session in our room. It was a potluck (sorry pot-bottle) party, as each person was supposed to bring one's preferred poison for the evening. We did arrange for some soft drinks, soda-water and snacks. Being penultimate day of our journey, everyone was ready to share one's experiences and was appreciative of the initiative taken by us (I and Pardeep) in calling for a memorable assembly. After a couple of hours, the gathering went for dinner and finally to their respective rooms dreaming about having had an adventurous and wonderful day.

View of the Oval shaped Tsomgo Lake

On our final day (7th day), after having morning tea, we packed our baggage for the return journey, and after having wholesome breakfast were ready to alight our assigned vehicles, which were already loaded with our baggage. The distance from Gangtok Hotel to Bagdogra airport is 125 Kms. Though the road is extremely good, it takes nearly 4-1/2 hours to reach the airport. The road is lifeline to Sikkim as most of the goods are carried from Siliguri. On way, we passed through Kalim Pong and one could identify directions to Bhutan and Bangladesh. There is a daily bus service from Siliguri to Bhutan. There is a road leading to Nepal. We were lucky to have a fast driver who dropped us at Bag Dogra airport in four hours, after we had started from Gangtok around 9.15 a.m. Before check-in we were able to have snacks. pre-screening. of baggage was done and we checked in and comfortably sat in departure lounge. The flight was on time, and we reached Delhi safely at around 6.45 in the evening. The coordinator collected and handed over our baggage and we bid farewell for the time being and promised to remain in touch after that as well. It was parting time after having enjoyed wonderful weeklong party time in happy company and at places full of fun. Narrating experience is perhaps, the only way to quench the lust for such adventures. I do hope all those who have read it, would have enjoyed it and that it would has left them for craving to have unlimited fun, which cannot be missed.

Before closing this chapter, I must add a couple of important places/events during our sojourn to Sikkim. Firstly, on our way from Darjeeling to Namchi, we halted at Lama Hatta. It used to be a marketplace for selling, among other things, cattle. It has been made picturesque by making a nice hill garden. It is a spot for taking pictures and some of us did so, especially Sudha Gupta felt like acting for a film shoot; Shahrukh style open arm pose, which brought out joy she was having at that place. In addition, we also had nice tea followed by tasty local oranges, which really diverted our minds from tiredness and also that we got some relaxation from really curvaceous and deep sloppy road. Likewise, on way to hotel in Namchi, we could also see a Football Stadium coming up. You have guessed it correctly that it has been named after famous footballer, Bhutia.

During our trip, we did not find people whiling away time. It seems, and it was confirmed too that people tend to find some job, however hard or small and that was why no Beggars were noticed anywhere. People there prefer to work hard and were even ready to carry heavy burdens on their backs. I wish elsewhere too this ideal could be followed elsewhere too!

I feel that my narrative would have awakened the urge to explore for oneself what one has been missing so far. I believe that such trips are not merely entertaining, educative but one finds that they uplift spirits and leave on longing to live longer and not miss anything in any corner of this world.

At the Confluence of River Indus (Sindhu and River Zanskar (blue) in Ladakh with Pradeep Gupta

3rd chapter

Ladakh - Not merely Land of Lamas at 75

Ladakh - Not merely Land of Lamas, Snow Desert but of Serene Natural Beauty

As mountains attract wandering clouds and cause happy rains, I too get attracted to mountains. I would not compare myself with Meghdoot of that great poet, Kalidasa, for there the Meghdoot - Cloud merely serves as Messenger of a Lover to His Beloved, in my case, I myself get attracted to the mountains and get the 'Shower of Complete Satisfaction'. Therefore, if in April 2017, I had travelled to the Northeast (Sikkim etc), in April 2018, I planned to visit Ladakh (19 to 26), where River Indus the very source of Indus Valley Civilization would be another main attraction. Yes, of course, I shall come again mount Yak and savour Yak Cheese. Meet simple Ladakhi people and give a treat to my eyes with the scenic and panoramic view of that Plateau, which definitely charms everyone without exception, I believed so, and I was no exception. I was excited like a child as the day of departure was coming near and I had in fact started dreaming of lakes and mountains. It was going to be another once-in-a- lifetime experience.

For the benefit of readers, I must share my experiences of my trip to Ladakh. As mentioned above, It was scheduled from Apr 19-26. I somehow recalled the old saying, " That man proposes but God disposes", when on the night of April 16 (just past mid-night) my mother (94 years) breathed her last. Though I had planned her care during my forthcoming short absence, it was then a different situation and a development that needed my immediate physical presence and also to take care of a number of things. Earlier, on March 30, 2018, she had expressed her last wishes in detail. These included that her last procession should commence from our house in Roorkee, which our parents had made. The cremation was to be done in Kankhal (Hardwar) and all the rites were to be performed by my nephew, her grandson, Gorav Bajaj, whose father (Ashok) had left us in 1998 itself. I wonder if she had foreseen her coming death and given responsibility to Gorav to tackle two issues with one stroke - remembering and honoring her son (our brother) and the second being sparing me from the duty of performing last rites so that the trip which I had planned in December 2017 should not in any way get disturbed. Was it merely a coincidence or her vision? My vote would be for the second. This credence was given by her leaving a left hefty sum for her rites and also for our maid Maya, who had been taking extra care of her 24 x 7 for the last 4 years. Mother was strong willed and mentally alert almost till her last breath. I feel humbled to have had such a great Mother.

After her last rites were performed on April 17, as per her wishes, naturally the question also arose, in close family gathering, on 18th April 2018, about my impending trip. While I had reconciled to drop the very idea of the trip, especially after its postponement or rescheduling was not worthwhile, my brothers advised me to go ahead with the trip, as it would provide me some distraction from mental trauma and also as my personal presence was not essentially a must - Gorav having been thrust with that. I did appreciate their right and sensible approach with modern outlook and their willingness to display their love to my desire to get a break. I did recognize that the world goes on as usual even after someone near and dear has departed. One does feel pain, experiences vacuum and misses the departed person but after a point, one has to reconcile and move on. Having had faced such a situation earlier also, when my wife Tripta met with a tragic and fatal accident on February 23, 2013, perhaps, I could muster strength easily to embark on my trip. Also, the ripe age of my mother and inevitability of death also gave me courage to live in the present.

Ladakh - Not merely Land of Lamas at 75

So as scheduled, I left for Leh on April 19 by Go Air accompanied by my friend, Pardeep Gupta (who was with me on my NE trip also and who had almost dropped the idea of going on the trip without me). More about my actual trip will follow, and, in the meantime, prelude to the trip should serve. I seek from my readers, their opinion about my decision to continue with the trip or was I ill-advised to do so. I am sure there will be divergent views, but I just want to see whether the majority supports my decision or stands opposed to it.

Taking the trip to Ladakh further, I may add that the flight to Leh was comfortable and reached Leh well within the scheduled arrival time. The sky was clear and blue. From the point of start in Delhi, it was the helping hand of my companion Pardeep Gupta, from check-in to check out, which made me relaxed but added to his responsibility, which he took in his stride and continued to extend help throughout the trip. He waited for me as and when required. He also literally gave me support to be able to walk, whatever little I could, and also kept the memories of the trip captured in his camera. He is also a keen traveller and photographer. Wanderer in him made me too to keep going on especially in a place like Ladakh, where lack of oxygen makes one breathless easily. He assured that we have preventive medication and even oxygen cylinder to cope with any emergency. Of course, evenings, sipping and gossiping and munching together made the tiredness of the day just vanish away and we used to have sound sleep.

On arrival in Leh, after collecting baggage, Gorav had made excellent arrangements for our reception, transport, meals, stay and even our medical check-up. It was reassuring and despite Gorav being engaged in his duties in Roorkee, he had made extensive arrangements kept a constant watch, and remained in touch, on the phone, throughout our stay to make our life easy and tension free. It was a home away from home, comfortable, cozy and welcoming. **At about the same time, when we had landed, another flight could not land as its wheel got jammed, but it should not scare anyone, for such freak incidents can happen** anywhere. The doctor after checking us thoroughly assured us that we were normally fit. He, however, advised us to get complete rest for the first day and also suggested that we take light meals and drink a lot of Luke-warm water to acclimatize faster.

He even suggested that it would be better if we could avoid hard drinks during our stay so as to prevent dehydration.

That day we finalized our detailed programme with Rin Zing, whom Gorav had arranged, and he proved to be our tour operator, taximan, guide, philosopher, jovial companion, and always ready to help and go out of the way to make us comfortable, and he did take extra care of me. We used to call him 'Rim Zhim' (raindrops) and he used to laugh. He could converse in Hindi very well and was a devout Buddhist. He would pray, bow, and always made it a point to show reverence to shrines and even made detour to show respect to any such symbol, monument, etc which he was supposed to follow. He was a man of few words but full of energy and a helping attitude. Above all, he followed rules and would not bend or circumvent them. Seeing that I have difficulty walking, he brought a self-made stick for me, which incidentally, I have brought back to Delhi as a memento. He also brought a local homemade brew 'Chang' when out of curiosity, we asked him about it. He said that Chang is taken by all in the family, to which they add barley 'Sattu'. They take Chang not as an intoxicant but for its nutritional values. I must endorse this concept or conviction. Ladakhi are physically fit people. They withstand harsh climates and shortages of oxygen easily. Greenery is less as it is dependent upon snowfall and the resultant water, including underground.

I believe that my readers are content with the journey to Ladakh and are really keen that I continue depicting my journey to Ladakh. However, before I continue, I may add a couple of pieces of vital information, which will be beneficial to know to equip oneself appropriately to have full satisfaction with the intended visit. Firstly, it is important to carry a post-paid phone. It is another matter as to who the service provider should be, since at different places, different networks provide better service. Overall, Airtel has a slight edge. Apart from the camera, binocular adds to adventure. For clothing and shoes, one needs to see weather forecast around the time of trip for it can be cold to very chilly. Also, flights for Ladakh do allow only 7 Kg handbag and with that limited weight in bag carrying camera, laptop, binocular, etc. becomes difficult.

Also, for going to interior places, like Nubra Valley, Pangong Lake etc. one is required to take an inner-line permit by applying in forms along with copies of ID proof at DC's office. After prompt checking, revenue is collected, and receipted permit is issued. It is advisable to make 4-5 copies of the permit, as it is required to be given at various check-posts. Another interesting factor, which came to light was that all taxi operators are required to pay Rs. 50/- to the Taxi Union on the day their services are hired. We were told that there are strict rules, and one is required to pay 20% of the booking charges to the Taxi Union, if taxis are hired through any of their members. To become a member, one is required to shell out a hefty sum of Rs. 50,000/-. What benefits, the union members derive was not clear but definitely there appears high and mighty behind this. Even at places of visit the taximen dare not cross the last point made for their stoppage and parking.

In the background is Old Shey Palace in Leh

While chalking out programme, I may add a couple of points which we gained from our experience. Firstly, the day of Sunday be kept for visiting Sangam (Confluence of rivers Indus and Zanskar) and on the way back to visit Gurudwara Pathar Saheb dedicated to the visit of Guru Nanak Dev ji. Army units take turns giving elaborate Lunger on Sundays and there is always a good congregation. Thereafter, one can visit the Ice Stupa, which is erected in January by throwing water on a structure, which lasts for 6 months or so. slowly, ice melts during summers and serves to irrigate crop fields. While in most parts of India, the wheat crop was being stood harvested, in Ladakh it was being sown then. Secondly, one should avoid making heavy trips in a row, like scheduling visit to both the mountain passes the same day to reach Nubra Valley and the Pangong Lake, as it adds to fatigue and should best be avoided. I must say that we had made enough preparations to start our roaming and romancing in Ladakh. Rin Zhin was always keen to take us to various Monasteries, Gompas, Stupas, Pagodas for he had faith in them, and naturally he wanted to show us how Lamas and other religious Gurus conduct themselves. For him, every place was sacred and important, with something different to offer by way of location, architecture, and the artefacts kept there. The Scenic beauty of each place was different, and routes were panoramic and captivating. Poplar type trees are abundant and provide the necessary wood for roofs etc. Wood carvings and bright colours definitely bring life to this mountain desert. One can find routes adorned with colourful flags and hangings and even walls have Mantras in script.

To make the travelogue more meaningful and easily comprehensible, I had requested that my friend Pardeep Gupta take photographs of the important places we visited and enjoyed together. Not only physically but mentally also, Pardeep lifted limping me. He motivated me to go on and encouraged me to make an extra effort, which indeed was helpfullp. In Ladakh, every hill gives one a different look and feel, for each one is different in colour and shape. One can come across various shades, hues and tinges of brown, black, grey, green, yellowish. Red, blue that one wonders about the beauty with which nature has adorned various places. Sand is aplenty. If I were to tell you that I was able to collect the best quality of Multani Mitti or Gachani for the best face pack of clay from near the roadside, no one would believe me but believe me so natural, light yellow Multani Mitti's quality was really excellent. Perhaps, we tend to ignore things which we get easily or freely. Be it water or pure air or even earth. Talking about colours, one will notice the difference in colours, e.g., water flowing in the River Indus and the River Zanskar. While, Zanskar water is deep blue, Indus water appears muddy. At the place of confluence, the visuals are eye-catching and soothing. The place is peaceful, and one rally wants to become a Yogi chanting in praise of God in whatever form, be it 'Om', 'Om Mani ...', 'Wahe Guru' or any other way or form.

The very first monastery we visited was perched on halfway up the hill and it gave such a peaceful and serene feel that made us realize as to what attracts many towards it. It is not that one is running away from day-to-day ordeal for I can foresee what a tough life resident of such monasteries lead. Keeping the place clean despite scarcity of water and living with scanty or limited variety, if not quantity, of food, means the place itself provides attraction and zeal to devote oneself to Him. Almost all religions, if not all, show that their Teachers, Gurus, Founders, Proponents, etc. did practise some kind of seclusion, meditated and got revelation about God and what He expects from human beings. In brief, nothing like self-realization! On way back from Pagoda we also saw the place near the River Indus for Maha Kumbh. In May and September, big festivals await Leh. Cultural troupes and local handicrafts are displayed. These are big attractions for visitors. Next, we visited Shey Palace- old Royal House. It looked in appearance like a muddy building and smaller in size in comparison to Leh Palace, which is a 9-storey building. However, both present a visual spectacle and view from top is really wonderful and especially from Leh Palace, the city view is clear and gives it a majestic look. Photographs are really eye-catching.

Without much side-tracking, I must continue with my trip to Ladakh, however, I would be failing if I did not to mention the excellent job being done by the Border Road Organization in making and maintaining all weather roads. Extensive coverage and excellent roads make us take pride in their work. Work is going on. Even the highest mountain pass boasts a motorable road. It is really hazardous work and to keep a constant watch about condition of roads and to maintain them is really tough job but being done with passion and devotion in tough weather and despite shortage of oxygen. All praise for their well-done job, as it ensures safety of the visitors there!

I have Resolved NOT to Stop

We did try local bakery items in a local Ladakhi House. It was something between bread and tandoori roti - with Buttered and Salted Tea. It was indeed refreshing. While tasting these things, we sat or squatted in Vjara Asana style on raised seats with low tables, which were beautifully carved and in flashy bright colours. Another noticeable thing about the house was 'huge collection of ornamental copper utensils and wares used to cook and serve food during festivities and celebrations and some for prayers'. The designs are theirs, but most of these utensils are made in Moradabad. We were greeted with a welcome smile, and our hosts felt honoured to receive and entertain us. Even children welcomed us with their traditional salute and smile though their shyness was visible. They wished us to stay longer so that they could attend to us in a better way, as we had gone literally unannounced, and tea was readily available. Hospitality was visible and meant to be extended, and not merely for demonstration, but caring and sharing are genuinely their way of treating visitors or guests.

Whatever I have written about Ladakh, so far, is based on my real experience without any exaggeration, and the trip indeed left a deep impression, and everything appears vividly clear, while I record it. I recall that in the morning when Rin Zhin used to come, he would call 'Julley' which means Thank You, please, but it is also used as a Greeting and said by taking the hand to the forehead in a salute style. To enquire 'how are we'; he would say 'Khamsang-in-a-Ley and taught us that to say 'I am fine' for which we were to respond by saying 'Khamsang-Ley' Another phrase especially when walking on a rough path, was 'Kule-Kule'. Easy to remember and really 'cool'. I recall that while in Tanzania, there in Swahili, for slowly, they used to call 'Pole-Pole'. Somewhat similar is the saying in Punjabi with tender touch. Another thing by using a word twice does not necessarily mean harshness, e.g. as in Hindi, 'Dhire-Dhire'. On our way back from Pagoda, we also saw the place near the River Indus for Maha Kumbh. In May and September, big festivals await Leh. Cultural troupes and local handicrafts are displayed. These are big attractions for visitors. Shey Palace- old Royal House- looks in appearance like a muddy building and smaller in size in comparison to Leh Palace, which is a 9-storey. However, both present a visual spectacle and the view from top is really wonderful, and especially from Leh Palace, the city view is clear and gives it a majestic look. Photographs are really eye-catching. It reminds me that we too await photographs for without visuals, words tend to become heavy and at times, relating them to the actual locale is not possible. I am therefore sticking to generalities or a general description of overall of Ladakh.

After a day's rest, on the 20th we headed for Hemis Monastry, which also has a museum, where artefacts, paintings, pots, ceramics and even skins of animals like the Snow Leopard and Panther adorn the walls, as these were gifted. A tusk, old coins, Tankha- wall hanging are other attractions and on way back we had stooped at Photang (Hemis Kumbh site). We also saw Stakna and Thiksey monasteries. Each one is different and quenches one's wandering lust. Our visit to a Ladakhi house has already been mentioned before as has been Shey Palace.

It would be worth recalling that in 2002 and 2003 respectively, the then PM and Deputy PM, Shri Atal Bihari Vajpayee and Shri Lal Krishna Advani, visited Sindhu Ghat near Kharu Village. The main building and its adage need proper upkeep; otherwise, it would not take long for them to vanish away, and the gained prominence will go into oblivion. Ladakh has also been locale for films like Highway, 3 Idiots, Bhag Milkha Bhag etc. but without any question, it was 3 Idiots, which brought Ladakh to prominence. Ever since, the flow of tourists has increased. So, we decided not to miss Rancho School. It is well spread, but pity is that we were not allowed to visit classrooms or interact with children, perhaps, with the idea of not wasting their time.

Start of Chilly yet Sunny morning at the Night shelter in Nubra Valley

At Pangong Lake with Pradeep Gupta

Some visitors did see the wall, which was used by one of the characters of 3 Idiots in a scene depicting urination. The school otherwise is spick and span, and in fact for using toilet facilities, a visitor is supposed to pay Rs. 10/-. There were adorned parking lanes just outside the school and a small gift shop on the compound. We also gathered that Mr. Rancho is settled in the US. He is also credited with harvesting water by making Ice Stupas. It seems that the whole of Ladakh always remains in a welcoming frame, as there is hardly a place which does not have busts, colourful flags, dhamma-chakras, etc.

The Evening was well spent discussing the day's venture, previous adventures and plans for future sojourns. Of course, the sundowner was always there to give us company. It had become somewhat chilly, and Kerosene Bukhari made the temperature, and our spirits rise, and we were looking forward to the day ahead with expectation and excitement, which, in turn, made us have a deep sleep.

The following day, after sipping warm water and having refreshed ourselves, we savoured tea in the comfort of our quilts, The night before, it had snowed, also but as there was no wind, the weather appeared fine. We knew that after the ice melts, the temperature will dip and in no way that was going to slow us down or disturb our programme for the day, which was to start after breakfast. Rin Zhin arrived at the appointed time, and after Julley, we packed for the day, as before, with warm and fresh water, juice etc. so as to keep away dehydration. Our first stop was the Hall of Fame maintained immaculately by the Army. A small entry fee brought us to the world of history, geography, bravery, gallantry, extreme sacrifice and valour. All those who had contributed to safeguarding and maintaining the sovereignty of India, stand glorified there. Apart from Jorawar Singh, who had won Ladakh to many who have been decorated with various gallantry awards find well described mention of their respective contributions. A place worth visiting and be one to one at least with photographs of such brave-hearted saviors. There is also a souvenir shop, and we chose to pick up a few articles, like Kargil Mug. After all, glorification is essential as it also motivates many more.

After the Hall of Fame, our next stoppage was at the DC's office to complete formalities with regard to the Inner line Permit for forthcoming travel crossing Passes. It did not take long and after making a few copies of the permit, we went to see Leh Palace. It had been destroyed in a fire and was rebuilt. One can have a clear view of the city from close to the Palace. From the roof top the entire valley presents a breath-taking scene. Impressive architecture and its location add to its charm.

Next on our schedule was Shanti Stupa. The Japanese style stupa reminded us of another somewhat similar stupa we had seen in Darjeeling last year. Not many people but that did not prevent its keepers from maintaining it sparklingly clean and shining. For people like me, the availability of a wheelchair was a big relief. The Stupa with its top high in the open sky made it look as if someone was in deep meditation without any care for the outside world. Ultimately, we have to find our inner self. On the way back, we stopped at the marketplace, and picked up a few artefacts, including a solar powered self-rotating ornamental prayer wheel to fit in one of the children's car. It was the last piece, so for other children, some other things were taken. Apart from locals, I could also see people from other regions owning shops. Most shops were owned by people from Kashmir Valley, who were owning shops with crafts andwoollens, like Pashmina, though being sold as Ladakh Pashmina, Yak Wool Jackets, Jewellery shops etc. There was a good crowd in the market and on top of that by the time we were returning a local musical group had started playing music. It was melodious. Somehow, I find much similarity in tune in almost all hill music. Is it a touch of Rag Pahadi? I do not know, but for sure, all the music in mountainous regions of India or even Nepal sounds similar to me having similarity. I leave it to knowledgeable people of music to let me enjoy the music itself.

At Shanti Stupa, Leh

On our way back, from the vegetable/fruit market, we picked up some vegetables and fruits, which understandably come from other parts of the state or even from Chandigarh. One could find bananas, melon, watermelon, cabbage, cauliflower, cucumber, carrots, Gourd and potatoes and the famous Kadam Sag (Ganth Gobhi), which is a delicacy of Kashmiri people. In the market, Ladakhi women were selling Onions, Coriander, Mint, Radish and some other local herbs. Our main aim was Gobhi - Cauliflower filled or stuffed Paranthas, the next day for breakfast and the fruits just for travel time. Gorav had made elaborate arrangements and had gotten supplies from Chandigarh. Locally, the prices were understandably just double and lacked the freshness of the plains. Some vegetables, of course, are also grown locally.

At the Magnetic Hill of Ladakh - Self and Pardeep.

We also saw from outside Apricot Oil Factory, as it was closed for then. Ladakh has the best quality of Apricot and especially the Kargil and Batalik areas are known for this. So Sweet, but at this time of the year we could only see blossoming apricot trees. Apricot oil is used for joint pain and is said to be effective. Another fruit is Leh Berry (somewhat smaller than but like Raisins) and its juice is considered full of antioxidants. For the present, we could find flowers on its thorny bushes. I will give more information on this a little later. We were advised that apricot oil on the market contains mostly refined oil and only a tinge of actual apricot oil. In July, hand ground oil, which is effective, is available. Shopping for dry fruits was kept for another day, which local ladies mostly sell. We passed by the local Tourist Office but could not find either a dedicated official nor much of literature. The Administration needs to promote this much more. In Sikkim and some other North-eastern States, we did find better arrangements.

We were excited over the line up for the next day, and after a relaxed evening and dinner and following news and a little bit of the IPL match, retired for the night.

The cloud burst of August 2012 and heavy rains caused heavy damage in Leh in which nearly 300 people got killed and property worth millions of Rupees got gutted. People remember that incident with a shudder. Hundreds of Shops and Houses had to be rebuilt. Rin Zhin showed us those areas which had suffered the most. It was Sunday the 22nd April, 2018 that we had kept for the Confluence of the Indus and Zanskar rivers. On the way we also saw the famous magnetic hill, where stopped cars in neutral gear automatically roll towards height. Almost every vehicle would stop and leave only after experimenting. There were no exceptions. People also ride Desert Bikes to have a deeper thrill. Before reaching the confluence from the top, visuals were worth watching. Rivers also serve to generate electricity. At many places, I also found solar panels and visibly awareness was spreading, and its importance was being well recognized and actually being practiced even in some of the pagodas. There is good scope for as sunlight is sharp, and to be comfortable, one needs to cover the eyes with goggles to safeguard from high glare.

I have Resolved NOT to Stop

So on Sunday 22nd April, we were at the confluence of the Rivers Indus and Zanskar. I have already described the feelings of peace, fulfilment and having achieved something worth remembering. The water was cool. It was sunny but a little breezy. Gorav had told me that had he been there he would have arranged a day long picnic with freshly prepared food and rafting. I can imagine the fun and enjoyment it would have added. But something must be left for the future and expectations. It gives life to one's passion and craving for creating something different and perhaps better. I collected some water, from the Indus River and I am sure, Mother would have appreciated that, for she used to enjoy sipping such holy waters, be it from the Ganga, Gurudwara Bangla Saheb or Baba Mandir in Nathu La. For the sake of memory, I would preserve it. At the confluence, hot tea was really enjoyable. After which we drove to a neighbouring village at a distance of 3 KMs, as Rin Zhin wanted to see his sister, who got married in that village and lo! she was washing clothes near roadside brook. His son also arrived on a sporty bike and got a hug and a reward of 100 rupees from his maternal uncle. He was happy and showed his skills on the bike as a demonstration of his skill and appreciation for the gift. Simple people, simple and straightforward life without any artificiality. After assuring himself of his sister's wellbeing, Rin Zhin drove a little farther to show us the marketplace and as if to tell us, the place where her sister stands married does not lack facilities. There were a number of eateries but they were empty. We were told that by the following month, visitors will start thronging eateries after visiting confluence. During our trip to Ladakh we found that Maggi is available even at the remotest of places and visitors like eating hot plates of Maggi in somewhat chilly weather. Of course, Dal and Rice, Noodles, Momos (or Dumplings) are other dishes. Served with Ketchup and at times with Green homemade chutney, one can have a fast, effective and economical response to hunger. Of course, traditional tea and normal tea are available. Cold drinks, chocolates are other favourites.

It was time to proceed to Gurudwara Pathar Saheb, on the way back which we had hurriedly passed while coming. I had mentioned the importance and its association with Guru Nanak Dev ji. On that day also, a jatha had come from Delhi (Tilak Nagar-Vishnu Garden side).

Everything was orderly, and the community feast Langar was well organized. Outside from Parking to collection of shoes, distribution and collection of Rumallas (essential head-covering) and distribution of Kada Prasad were machine like but full of devotion and fervor. After getting blessings and langar Prasad, we proceeded to see the Ice Stupa and another monastery nearby.

At Patthar Saheb Gurudwara in Leh

I had described the Ice Stupa earlier and said that it is a man-made structure built every year. It is the very idea of making it and preserving water for use when needed most that makes it different and deserve praise for very thought to make something different and useful. The Monastery of course was one at expectedly secluded place and required some effort by the devotee to reach it and receive its blessings. It was really a day of visiting holy places as our next stop was the famous Kali Mandir with red flags visible from a distance. Visible from the roadside often passed by us frequently, on a hilltop leaves a message of empowerment. The face of main idol remains covered barring two days of rituals annually. Lamas and not Pandits serve there. Elaichi Dana (sweetened Cardamom) the traditional prasad is given. Since the next day's plan was to start as early as 5 am, we came for overnight rest but only after our heartful meal, similarly, as that very morning before starting we had enjoyed Gobhi (Cauliflower) Paranthas with excellent curd, pickle, butter and tea. We realized later on that suddenly our diets had got a Philip and we had become glutton. Cold climate, healthy water and roaming had indeed increased our digestion and we were enjoying every morsel we used to take.

I do not know whether it was just a wanderlust or nature calling in its embrace, but I always feel refreshed whenever I am close to it. Lure of nature in its prime catches my imagination and I get really charged up. Whenever I am close to nature, I feel that I am close to Him and He takes on from thereon. I must have been in wilderness in my earlier incarnation, I believe and perhaps that is why lust is there to revisit such places. We had well prepared ourselves for April 23, as it was one of the highlights of the tour and for that I had taken the medicine (1 tablet twice daily) recommended by the doctor and also advised in the Sheet of Information given by the Tourist Office. To be extra careful we also took a small-size Oxygen Cylinder for Rs. 650/- and if not used only Rs. 100/- was to be deducted, fair enough. We kept warm water, tea in thermos and sandwiches for breakfast on the way. The destination was Pangong Lake after crossing Chang La pass 17688 ft second highest motorable pass in the world. For us it was going to be historic. The road generally is good and patchy for a few kilometres from the pass either way. During peak of summer when ice melts, travel on the road becomes even more difficult. One has to be a good and careful driver with extraordinary negotiating skills, with full caution and attention on the road. As Ring Zhin's own vehicle for the purpose was held up in Kashmir Valley by the protestors, he had to take his friend with his own vehicle on the trip. It was like a bonus to us for Ring Zhin could explain to us various places on way and he made us stop at places with picturesque view. He showed us last village Tagir on way to Chang La, which has cultivation. We arrived Chang La pass without any trouble and stopped there for quick use of toilet and most importantly to photo record the event of having successfully arrived there.

One of the 3-Idiot Chairs at Pangong Lake

From Leh it is 36 KMs up to Kharu Village and another 45 KMs to Chang La and 30 KMs downhill to Durpuk and further 38 KMs lies the Lukhung the starting point of Lake Pangong. Real Bravehearts guard and maintain check post and path to reach and cross here whereas we hardly spent any time. There was no trouble encountered by us as we had limited physical exercise or even walking. We were advised to take long breaths and also take Luke-warm water and most importantly, no one should be allowed to doze as it can create problems and even be fatal. We came across frozen river, Sulta and after going a few KMs downhill, Pardeep and Ring Zhin indeed walked on it and pretended to be skating. Between Chang La and Durpuk medical facilities are available courtesy of the Armed Forces. We also came across unpredictable Pagla Nala - a stream which changes course just 3 KMs before the lake.

We were able to see Yaks grazing and Mountain Rodents and also a few birds. On way to the Lake, Pangong we stopped to have something to eat after we saw in the valley a lone hut with welcoming sign of an eatery near a water body, as in Durpuk the eateries were still shut. We were able to take freshly made Maggi and Tea to give our tummies some respite. The journey had really made us hungry. Ms. Tshering, the owner of the place gladly accepted being photographed. While serving Maggi, she said Don-Lay, meaning please eat. At the end we were tutored by Ring Zhin to say Shimpo Ruk-Lay and Julley Dangs-Ley, describing 'It was delicious and Thanks and that I was full'. Finally, we like the 3 Idiots arrived at Lake Pangong. Clear Blue water

I have Resolved NOT to Stop

of the lake was really breath-taking - so serene and pristine! Kareena's yellow scooter, which she had mounted in the movie was lying there as it was bought by an entrepreneur for Rs. 1 Lakh, who used it for people getting selfies on it for a fee of Rs. 50/-. I sat on one of the three colourful chairs but could not tell with which of the 3 Idiots, I should be identified. Of course, I took the opportunity to ride on a decorated Yak for a small fee of Rs. 50/- and near the lake, it was quite thrilling. Pity is, in India lies only a small portion of the lake and the rest is in China. People prefer to enjoy overnight camping there to watch the clear sky and stars. However, we took the advice of returning for lack of oxygen for overnight or in an emergency as at the height of 14000' it can pose problems. There are abundant eating jaunts but at that time they were virtually abandoned. So, for our food, we decided after spending meaningful and enjoyable time at the lake and going a little farther to return back. On the way we had a lunch of Momos and noodles and topped it with tea. The place was sunny but chilly because of the wind. We also learned that another way also goes to Nubra Valley, which was our destination of the following day. People do take that route to save time of travelling to and from Leh, but we preferred not to venture and give ourselves some rest, especially our lungs and legs.

One good thing in Ladakh is that there is effective plastic ban. The lake area was also clean and sparkling water of the lake was inviting. On way back we hardly stopped at the pass and drove back to have a quite evening and be ready the next day around 9 for our next adventure.

Wearing the Himachal Cap at Pangong Lake

The Himachal Cap I wear, particularly in photographs taken at the confluence of the River Indus and River Zanskar (deep blue water) was gifted to me by Pardeep, and I wore this colourful cap to match the colourful scene at the confluence. These are not mere words of encouragement in my narration of the visit, such instances really make anyone satisfied and motivated to do justice to the surroundings. I am also trying to keep in mind that there will be many like me, wish or even plan to visitvisit Ladakh for the first time. Believe me, the place should not be missed at all and there can be no two opinions about it. In 1962, Close to Pangong Lake, Indian Forces had to face Chinese aggression. Chang La (La in it means Mountain Pass) has been on route of travellers to China since ancient times.

On 24th morning we were fresh after deep slumber and after having a hearty breakfast, we were again ready for that day's programme and as usual Ring Zhin arrived on appointed time and once already packed overnight bags and a few other things for the way were put on his friend's car, we started on our journey. The road throughout the journey was good and the journey was smooth. On April 24, 2018, our journey to Khardung La took us to South Pullu Check Post 28 at the height of 15300' and we crossed Khardungla at the height of 18300'. In a temple there one can hear devotional songs. The usual precautions were taken and after brief photo session, we proceeded ahead trouble-free and with satisfaction of having crossed the highest motorable pass. There are people, who dispute its actual alleviation and argue it is less than 18300'. Be it so, if at all, we were there not to create any world record or set an example of human endurance, we were merely crossing it for our own sake and enjoyment and have a grand view and to salute those who had made it possible for people like us to pass by it. Those guarding our frontiers need appreciation and recognition. Unarguably, such passes had made travel easier and faster for centuries and if such routes had not been discovered, we would have remained unknown for a great time even to our Neighbours. It is also true that such mountain passes had helped not only traders but also invaders. But if everything had only positive results, the world would have been quite different. As it is said that thorns also grow with flowers and fruits - a little later on that too.

I have Resolved NOT to Stop

After crossing highest Motorable pass Khardungla (18300') at North Pullu Check Post.

After crossing Khardungla, the North Pullu Check Post, which is also at the height of 15300, the copies of the Inner line Permits were deposited. Incidentally, the permanent residents of J&K are not required to obtain such permits. Khardungla is named after the name of Khardung Village. Pullu is like a temporary shelter or Dera for the shepherds. The road is very good, and we were able to cover a distance much faster than on the Lake Pangong side and what we had imagined. We crossed villages and Bastis, like Khalsar and Disket to reach the mountain desert Hundar in Nubra Valley. Gorav had made arrangements for our night stay and after check-in and after enjoying Maggy again for getting fast relief to our hunger, we were ready to confront with Bactrian Double-hump camels. In mountainous desert, these prove a real help to carry goods. While Yaks help in hilly routes, these camels help in sandy areas. River was flowing slowly, and each camel ride cost Rs. 150/- for a small round of about 15 minutes. For cleanliness purpose the camels are kept in a marked area only. They have thick growth of hair like Yaks. Almost hairy body like bears. Color of course is brownish. Among other things, these camels can eat the leaves of thorny bushes of Leh Berry, which are in abundance there. Leh Berry is considered highly antioxidant and liked by all. Leh Berry is sold in factories for making juice and jam at a high price of Rs. 430/-

a Kg but to collect even two Kgs of Leh Berry from thorny bushes one has to spend the entire day and struggle with thorny bushes. There are more pricks than tiny fruit. But if it were not rare, it perhaps, would not have caught human imagination of being a delicacy.

Self (R) and Pardeep Gupta (L) with Double Hump Camel in Nubra Valley

Pardeep also pointed to a mountain, which appeared shiny black. He enquired us as to what we think of that mountain and while we thought it to be a rocky mountain or at best salt rock, he said it was likely to be Shilajit. We could believe it, as Ladakh is also known for it. After that, we drove to a neighboring village and among other things, also bought Dry Yak Cheese. It is hard to bite but like a Betel Nut slowly one can go own sucking and chewing it. It is both nutritious and a good pastime, like eating groundnuts by opening shells during travel. Like Chewing Gum, one may imagine, but it is salty not sweet. There was also a performance of local artists with masks. After our evening enjoyment over drinks and having had dinner, it was time to go for a deep sleep-in mountain valley with a clear sky and light murmur of water in cozy and comfortable bed. The next day (25th April) after a hot bath and satisfying breakfast, we were ready to have our explorations on penultimate day of our trip.

I have Resolved NOT to Stop

Naturally, the day in Ladakh cannot start without seeking Lord Buddha's blessings, so we also took shelter of Distek Monastery with its impressive Budha Statue in the open in a mountainous Valley with a panoramic and breath-taking view and of course looking at serene and peaceful surroundings. Each moment was blissful!

Having heard of hot springs in the area, Gorav told Ring Zhin that we must be taken there. For him too it was an exploratory trip. However, we arrived at the place, but before that I noticed a bakery and prompted and prodded Pardeep to try the local bakery. He jumped at the idea and bought cake and freshly baked biscuits. Just for Rs. 130/- both were unimaginable. After all, we arrived at the hot spring, after first confusing ourselves with privately owned places, which would have been a costly affair. Without any directional signboards and almost hidden but reachable by car paramik was our real destination, developed by Leh Development Authority, Paramik. Hot springs turned out to be another high point of the entire trip. These are maintained and kept in good running condition by the Self Help Group of Women (Women Alliance Panamin), who in groups of two, take turns to do their duties of maintaining separate bathing pools for ladies and gentleman, where temperature can be monitored to maintain a pleasantly tolerable temperature for human bodies. They have changing rooms also. After a good and enjoyable bath and after having changed, it was time to enjoy hot tea with items brought from the local bakery. Believe me, on hilltop, after bath on a sunny but windy day, the tea was like Nectar of Life and hunger having started knocking, the tea and bakery items turned out to be a big relief as for sure both tea and bakery were tasty and matched our tastebuds. On top of that entry to that place and cost of tea was pitiably low, beyond our imagination or expectations. I wish that a little more attention to notify the place and signboards should make the place a good tourist attraction. Somehow, we are not able to market or sell our places and products, as people in foreign countries are able to do.

Absorbing the fresh air enroute

Not only lack of infra-structure (which was not the case here), shyness to glorifying our places of history and natural beauty is perhaps need of the hour, to be rectified. If we have to follow the vision of PM of India to make India a top tourist hub, much more needs to be done, but which requires not huge funds but sheer imagination and a little effort. It was time for us to say good-bye to Nubra Valley and after crossing Khardungla without any difficulty, we reached Leh safely. However, before heading for our place of stay, we went to see Gurudwara Datun Saheb of whom we had heard at the Pathar Saheb Gurudwara. It is also associated with Sri Guru Nanak Dev ji, who's tiny Datun (Miswak toothbrush) is supposed to have grown as a huge tree over years. The tree there was really thick and tall. If the day had started with getting blessings from Lord Budha, the evening was well spent to take blessings of Sri Guru Nanak Dev ji to flourish like the Miswak Datun.

We could not resist the temptation to pick up freshly baked bread when in a nearby bakery we saw it being made and a good aroma was in the air. Am I the only one who thinks of food and at those different foods, all the time. I wish to try everything and all through had been doing so. Any remote place or any item called specialty of a place or shop attracts me and I cannot stop. For sure, I had found wonderful and tasty stuff at small and remote places. After reaching our place and retiring for the evening provided good relief from the tiredness of the day-long journey. Time was coming close to say good-bye to Leh. In the meantime, with me take dreams of all the wonderful days spent there.

Yak Ride at Pangong Lake

On April 25, before returning home, we made it a point to visit market specially to buy dry fruits. Dry apricot, black berries, walnuts we picked up for sharing with friends. One pair of woollen colorful socks, I picked up for my daughter. I know it was summertime, when woollens were not required but inner cloth lining in socks and design and also the price of just 200/- rupees were reasons enough to pick at least one pair. I also wanted to go for Yak Wool half-coat but stocky as I have become, finding the right size proved a problem. Otherwise, the design and the price were to my liking. I know I am compulsive buyer as at times I become extravagant, if I like something and at the same time I am stingy, counting every dime and haggling over price. .Likewise, at times I do not care about quantity I buy for it can go waste but perhaps I get satisfaction of buying especially things like vegetables and fruits in quantity and in my mind, I think that in a way I am helping the sellers of these things. My late wife used to chide me on my habit but after all, it had become a habit and as the saying goes, old habits die hard. At least I was living my way and was amply satisfied.

At Second Highest Motorable Pass - Changla (17688')

Self and Pradeep Gupta at Pangong Lake

Finally came April 26, the day scheduled to return back home. At times one is eager to return home, but this was exactly not so. However, there were commitments back home and obligations to take care of. It might be recalled that I had left before certain rituals with regard to Mother's demise were to be performed on April 28, which after returning on april 26 to Delhi and coming to Roorkee on April 27, I could very well attend to. That is exactly what I had done. On April 26,

I have Resolved NOT to Stop

the Go Air flight was on time. We packed our bags and after having brunch left for the airport around 09:30 hrs. and covered short distance up to the airport quickly. After formalities efficiently done by airport and airline staff, we waited shortly for the flight. The back home journey was trouble free. The driver was there to pick us up. I persuaded Pardeep that I should drop him at his place in Gurgaon as there was a direct route from there to our place. A slight detour will at least provide us some more time to chat and enjoy mentally time happily and enjoyably spent in Ladakh. As they say 'Ladakh Maa Ldemo Duk-Ley' that "Ladakh is beautiful", perhaps, it is time for my readers to go there and say 'Julley'. After all, mere imagining the beauty of a place, goodness of people and a Dream Come True is not possible. It has to be given a practical shape and I have no doubt that, in turn, you might be able to find what you had always dreamed of.

I have Resolved NOT to Stop

Remembering Capt Sourabh Kalia over beer while sitting in Revolving restaurant at Palampur

4th chapter

In the lap of Dhauladhar, Palampur at 76

Visit to Kayakalp, the Bundle of Health

While we were on our tour of Ladakh, I could find that my slow pace was caused by my being overweight. Though my friend Pardeep had been extending help I needed, he told me that I must overcome this difficulty and suggested that I should spend 10 days in Kaya Kalap of Palampur, which I had been dilly-dallying. However, as a true well-wisher he never left persuading me to the extent of coaxing me. Pardeep Gupta came to my place on the return from another engagement and took a solemn promise from me that I would, no longer put off my visit to Palampur. He not only narrated his own experience there but also ensured that I complete all the necessary pre-departure formalities then and there. Taking his sane advice and help, I reserved my train tickets from Delhi to Pathankot, as well as reservation in Kaya Kalp. Another thing, which made my decision easier was his offer that he too would not only be in Kaya Kalap but would also ensure to pick me up by his car from Pathankot and drop me on completion of our stay. Not only it appeared lucrative but further rising heat of NCR, offered me a good excuse to escape to a Hill Station, like Palampur. So, I started dreaming of total Kaya Kalap trip from 7th to 17th May, 2019.

Precisely, Kaya Kalap is in Holta (Palampur) and it is managed by Vivekanand Medical Research Trust) brainchild of once HP's Chief Minister Shanta Kumar. There is an airport near Palampur (around 30 Kms), known as Dharamshala or Kangra. There is also an overnight Volvo Bus of Himachal Tourism, which plies between Delhi (ISBT) and Palampur.

I have Resolved NOT to Stop

Assured of comfortable travel, I did embark on my journey-cum-adventure on 6th May, 2019 from Nizamuddin Railway Station by Jhelum Mail. The train was late by over an hour, but the overnight journey was comfortable and true to his word, Pardeep was at the station Pathankot - Chaki Bank near River Vyas to pick me up. We went to the Forest Rest House and had much needed tea and after having freshened up and having had sumptuous Brunch embarked on our journey to Palampur. Close to the Rest House there were blooming Jacaranda trees, reminding me of my days in Harare (Zimbabwe) and instantaneously, I recalled that a poem I had penned on Jacaranda, which I shall try to repeat later on. The hilly tract and curvaceous route had started. The cool breeze was soothingly welcome. On way, Pardeep would narrate various landmarks and describe their importance. On way we stopped to have fresh and refreshing cane juice laced with fresh mint, lemon and ginger. Really refreshing and mouth savouring. It quenched the thirst. He also pointed to Nurpur, his ancestral town and also mentioned that there was an Agricultural University, where he had studied, on way to Palampur. He also explained that agricultural research has helped farmers to grow a lot more vegetables and in fact, on way after every short distance we found vendors of fresh vegetables and fruits. He also mentioned that Nurpur takes its name from Mughal Queen Noorjahan, who had fancied spending the summer months there. Also, there was a Krishna temple with a tall black marble statue of Krishna, which was brought from Chittorgarh by the local King and understandably it was the one which legendry Mira used to worship, "Pad Ghungroo Bandh Mira Nachi Re."

At Kayakalp, Holta, Palampur

In the lap of Dhauladhar, Palampur at 76

After a pleasant long drive, we reached Palampur and completed admission formalities and had our first meal there before entering my room, as Pardeep could get booking only from May 9. There were various residential blocks, and I was accommodated in Block, Niket on twin-sharing basis and as per my request on ground floor, as also as close as possible to other facilities. The room was both quite spacious, neat and clean, as also equipped with attached bath, and with all the essential gadgets, including a TV/telephone.

The room which I got had beautiful view of snow-capped mountain range of Dhauladhar. The whole complex has been landscaped tastefully. It boasts of grass and various trees with blossoming flowers. There were creepers, flower plants and trees. There were also small well-shaped rain-water harvesting structures. The complex also had a number of solar panels and was apparently self-sufficient in electricity generation. There were separate buildings for the residential complex, library/lecture hall, evening meditation centre, for food and treatment etc. The buildings were named in Hindi and in itself described as to what each one of them contain, e.g. Eating place was Annapurna; Meditation Centre was Dhayan Mandir, Treatment Block was Niramaya, etc. At the time of admission, one gets a record-book, which eventually details, treatments, ailment history, medication, diet plan and discharge instructions etc. One also gets a handy bag containing timetable for various events, shower cap, towel and sheet for personal use ensuring hygiene. A charge of Rs. 500/- was taken as Registration. Room and almirah keys were given. However, the house-keeping staff keeps extra keys for daily cleaning of rooms/bathrooms and change of towels, linen, etc.

As promised above, hereby I reproduce Jacaranda poem penned by me on Zimbabwe's Silver Jubilee Celebrations of Independence (Date: 17-03-2005) and had recited it during their National Day Reception in Delhi.

"I have travelled far and wide
And seen strife and divide
Has earth no such place

I have Resolved NOT to Stop

Where one finds peace and solace
Reminisce, it used to be under blooming Jacaranda tree,
Where I used to find freshness in body and mind free
What a nice it used to be the scene
Full of fragrance and everything looking serene
What an ornamental plant
Which used to enchant
For miles lines of trees with blooming flowers
As if God has painted violet natural tree towers.
Intermittently petals would fall,
As if nature welcoming in its arm, I recall
It was Harare that I first saw nature's gift
Believe me I got spell bound and magic was swift
So very attractive that I would not like to leave
An eye-catching scene, if you believe
I was told 'Jacaranda' is the native of the West Indies and South America
It found shelter and perfect home in Africa
It got proper nurture and atmosphere.
Which made to enhance its beauty here
Like my own brethren from my own land
Who left to live in Zimbabwe, hand -in- hand
Like Jacaranda they were accepted and blossomed there
It became their home and never thought to move elsewhere
Then Harare was Salisbury and Zimbabwe, the Southern Rhodesia
The British used to rule, major parts of Africa and Asia
India had started the freedom movement and got independence.
It inspired many others to start getting rid of the dominance.
From British rule freedom was won
Apartheid and Racial discrimination got a shun
Efforts of thousands of freedom fighters got paid,
And path for progress got laid
Be close to nature, care for environment
Grow more trees, from a Niaanga* I had learnt

Who had told me, souls of my forefathers seek,
That I should grow more trees, to find my peak
By giving us Jacaranda, God did open its kitty
And for this we must be grateful to the Almighty
Trees bring health and calm, so grow more trees like Jacaranda.
At least I have come to know of this Funda".
* *Niaangas are Village Doctors there.*

The next day, at 5 in the morning, like others, I too was given tepid warm water to drink and freshen up after a while. At 6 we assembled for a Yoga Class followed by Pranayam (Breathing Exercises) and Laughter Session. Of course, we were also made to practice Jal Neti and Rubber Neti, the exercises to cleanse Nostrils and make breathing smoother. There were exercises for eyes and ears. It was one hour's session. I gather that people come from as far as Chennai in India and a couple of foreigners also came from abroad. Quite a few were repeaters and assured me that they did benefit from the past visits.

At Baijnath's Lord Shiva's Temple

After this we came to our respective rooms for taking bath etc. and thereafter to have breakfast we came to Annapurna. The regimen of food was really very strict and the staff there served strictly according to one's prescribed diet. It used to be balanced for carbohydrates, fats, salts and sugar. It included seasonal fruits and there were strict instructions for Number of Chapatis or even milk. There used to be various kinds of Chutneys, Soups, Tea etc. However, every detail was prescribed in the Diet Chart of each person. For the first day, one was required to consult the doctor, who after through check-up knowing problem and history would prescribe the line of treatment, which included various massages, baths - cold and hot, medicine, if required, and of course detailed dietary plan. After which one would to the rooms where prescribed treatments were available and each patient would get the required treatment. In the afternoons the doctors were available for prescribing the following day's course of treatment.

If required one could take bath and come for Lunch, as prescribed. Afternoons a couple of hours were free to take rest. In the evening there used to be an assembly for meditation. One of the doctors was also available in the evenings, to give a briefing on various regimens, explain benefits as also to answer any specific query of any patient. One could also enjoy game of table-tennis or walk on stony path to serve as acupressure and people used to assemble in parks to chit-chat and exchange views, as also to know each other more closely. Fruits and tea were available. Like Lunch, Dinner timings were also fixed. Thereafter people could for walk or talk. As per one's choice, people used to retire for the night. Some patients were given milk and raisins before they would go for sleep. Everything was prepared from fresh supplies and freshly. No one was allowed to waste food but was required to follow the dietary restrictions.

Pardeep arrived as scheduled accompanied by his companion and after that we really used to have a gala time. so, after taking proper permissions, we went out to attend marriage of Pardeep Friend's son. I too was curious to witness a Himachali marriage in Himachal Pradesh itself. The venue was in the midst of a tea garden and gave us excuse to indulge in enjoying lavish dishes and even drinks. Pardeep explained to me that these days, lavish display of dishes has become common whereas earlier there used to be restrictions and simplicity. It was only past mid-night that we could return to Kaya Kalap.

At Sobha Singh's Art Gallery, Palampur

After a couple of days, we again sought permission to go out to see the famous Bajnath Temple, which is dedicated to Lord Shiva and people come there to offer prayers in good numbers. Although there was a big que, we were allowed from a side door to enter. I could see among other offerings there were also Whitish and bell shaped Dhatura flowers. This Bajnath is different from one in Bihar and yet another in Uttarakhand. Although apparently there is a similar story of Ravana having brought Mount Kailash and because of an urgent urge to pass water, having to hand over the Mount Kailash to someone else, but as was ordained, once it was put to rest by the other person, the Shiva in Linga form got firmly rooted there. Ravana could do nothing to take it. Incidentally, during Dussehra Festival, effigy of Ravana is not burned here. After all, Belief over time get even more firmed up.

There were eateries, cold drink sellers and even sweetmeat sellers besides local artefacts and articles for prayers. We did make good use of time in enjoying there. After this we went to see the famous Art

I have Resolved NOT to Stop

Gallery of famous Artist, Sobha Singh, who has painted Sikh Gurus and a few others, like leaders, Soni Mahiwal, etc. The work is displayed there for which there is a fee, and also a shop, which is owned and run by his son and daughter-in-law. They sell replicas, reprints, jams, pickles, clothes, etc. It is not a very large estate, but upkeep is tidy. There were also various plants and fruit trees, like Litchi. One can also see his studio and his belongings on first floor, which can be reached by climbing narrow but steep stairs.

Making most of it one day, we go out to see tea gardens, purchase famous Kangra Tea with a nice aroma and a reasonable price of Rs. 300/- for a Kg. We enjoyed chilled beer in a Restaurant, located near a brook, which Capt Saurabh Kalia used to frequent, before his body was mutilated by Pakistani soldiers, when unfortunately, he lost his way, while on patrol duty at the border. My big Salute to that Immortal and Braveheart of India.

Dhauladhar hills in the backdrop of Kayakalp, Palampur

How could we miss the famous Revolving Restaurant in Palampur? One afternoon, we again got permission so that we could enjoy our drinks and dinner there. We also enjoyed the evening lights of the city and Pardeep dutifully explained to me various landmarks of Palampur. Indeed it was another pleasant evening and both food and bill there were to our liking.

Despite, going a little wayward, while in Kaya Kalap, I lost 3 Kgs. in weight, which definitely could have been more if I were not tempted by other thrills. Believe me, the total bill of Kayakalap was just Rs, 27,000/- for ten days stay, food, various treatments and that in a hill station during summers.

As per promise, Pardeep dropped me off at Pathankot but only after we enjoyed our lunch on the way and his friend also gifted us Mushrooms, which I enjoy a lot. Pardeep ensured that I was comfortably lodged on my berth and after a safe journey reached home. Kaya Kalap, though was no less than a home with all the needed care.

We have such jewels at many places, and I would definitely advice not to miss such places. There is nothing to lose except excess fat and weight, while there are enormous benefits to be reaped.

I have Resolved NOT to Stop

View of Kibber village at 14,010 ft. It is the base for visitors to the Kibber Wildlife Sanctuary, home to about 30 snow leopards

5th chapter

Dev Bhumi, Himachal Pradesh at 76

Adventure Aplenty - Kinnaur and Lahul/Spiti with High Passes of Kunzam and Rohtang.

When the sultry weather after heavy rains started making me dull in NCR Delhi during July 2019, naturally there arose a growing urge to go to some cooler place. One or two showers did provide some relief, yet my yearning for rushing to the hills could not be curbed. The reality is that the lure of hills is always overpowering, and distant/remote places excite me even more. That is why I had planned to go to Kinnaur and Lahaul/Spiti in Himachal Pradesh. My dear friend, Pradeep Gupta and his son, Chandan readily joined. Pradeep, who is originally from Himachal Pradesh, drew the itinerary keeping in mind my interests and also arranged for our night shelters. Having been retired as a Divisional Forest Officer in Himachal Pradesh, he very well knew as to what was best and economical for us and moreover took care of booking an Innova with a Himachali Driver, keeping necessarily in mind safety on hilly tracks. He even booked my train ticket from Delhi to Chandigarh in Kalka Shatabdi on July 29. His son Chandan was to join from New Delhi Railway Station. We had each other's phone numbers and having exchanged that we should meet in front of the reserved coach that is what we actually did. Chandan arrived as scheduled and we exchanged pleasantries. The train arrived on time, and we settled down in our seats. It was a good omen that our train started on time. As we had met for the first time, we exchanged notes on each other. It was trouble-free journey and courtesy, Indian Railways we were served snacks and tea.

After reaching Chandigarh Railway Station, the driver Sunil Thakur, who had come from Shimla took us to Pradeep's residence in Omaxe Complex in New Chandigarh. Yes, of course Pradeep was constantly on the phone enquiring about progress of our journey. I could feel myself excited about the journey onward. After arriving at Pradeep's place before retiring for the night we enjoyed our drinks and had a sumptuous dinner, and we also discussed the plans for our onward march. We decided to leave at 0900 hrs the following day after breakfast. It was time for bed and the end of the first day. To add to my excitement, Pradeep showed me some photographs, which indeed served as a precursor and glimpse of what was going to unfold further on our actual journey.

After having slept trouble-free, I got up fresh in the morning and after attending to my morning natural calls, three of us were at the dining table to devour a heavy breakfast. Sunil, the driver, was also accommodated by Pradeep in his luxurious flat and was ready at the appointed time. The baggage was packed, and I was privileged to occupy the navigator's seat next to the driver. Our destination for 30th July was Rampur and precisely the night stay was at the Forest Rest Camp in Nogli, near the river Sutlej.

The first 115 Kms distance up to Shimla via Kalka were absolutely trouble-free. The roads were being widened and once in a while there would be drizzle. Although we were advised to stagger our trip by a fortnight in view of possible road blockages and landslides, yet having got feedback through trustworthy friends of Pradeep that there was no major problem being visualized, we kept the original plan. On our way we passed by the famous Giani Dhaba but it did not have the same look as it used to give in the past, where I had enjoyed good meals earlier. Forlorn and depressing, it appeared for it would be demolished in the process of much essential widening of roads. I have always believed and found the people of Himachal being docile, well-behaved, trustworthy, loyal and hard working. During this journey too my conviction was reinforced when one unknown driver requested our driver to hand over some important documents to his dear ones on our way. At the exact stop, our driver could locate the person and handed over the documents. That is the kind of simplicity and trustworthiness. I wish it could be spread, and the very thought of cheating gets buried deep and forever.

After crossing Shimla, we were on the way to Narkanda via Kufri (15 Kms); Fagu (6 Kms.) and another 40 Km to Narkanda. By the time we reached Fagu it was decided to have Lunch, as the traffic had become slow due to heavy fog and trucks loaded with fruits, mostly apples, for Mandis in Chandigarh and Delhi. The fog did somewhat dampen our spirits, and we were apprehensive as to what was in store for us. The driver encouraged us by saying that it would be like that up to Narkanda only, and once we cross Narkanda, we should have a better view of scenic beauty. Lunch turned out to be ordinary but could relieve us from hunger though it was rather tongue-burning hot. I was told that the Apple Orchards were first planted by Mr. Stokes, an American, who had married and settled in this area. His daughter, Vidya Stokes, was Speaker of the Himachal Pradesh Assembly for a long time. The others took plantations of apples from Mr. Stokes and today Himachal boasts of delicious apples and has transformed the economy of Himachal. It provides employment to many from farming aid, shopkeepers of farming tools and other implements, fertilizers and insecticides, as well as cooperative marketing societies and transporters. Today, HP, has plantations of not only apples but also pears, plums, apricot and now, recently cherry. Walnuts and Pine Nuts are also aplenty. Grapes and Pomegranates are also on the rise. Except at one spot and that too for a couple of minutes we could enjoy open view of sky and were able to click otherwise it remained foggy up to Narkanda, exactly as was mentioned by our Driver. During that opening, we were able to see colourful houses perched in distant hills and winding roads. Of course, we could always feel lush, green, towering trees surrounding us. The traffic though not much, it needed safe driving. Our lungs had started feeling the freshness of cool air. Rampur was the seat of Late Raja Vir Bhadra Singh, former Chief Minister of Himachal. On arriving at the Night Shelter, we found the Caretaker approaching us. It was a nice and cozy place next to the river

Sutlej and we could hear the murmur of water. After freshening tea and washing, we settled down for our evening drinks - more a ritual than a habit and specially to enjoy company and prepare plans for the forthcoming journey.

Before retiring for the day, we had a simple but delicious dinner. Especially, the beans were fresh and tender, and on top of that, rightly cooked, neither overdone nor half done. The night was spent dreaming for the activities of the following day, as I was told that it would be a very important highlight of our tour. On wakening up and after having made us ready for breakfast, it was decided to have breakfast in the open yard of the Rest House, so as to enjoy the scenic setting of the night shelter and also to enjoy listening to murmur of River Sutlej. It was a real adventure while enjoying a hot breakfast in bearable light cold, made the setting even more enchanting. Oh! I had forgot to mention that it was another 66 Kms from Markanda to Rampur.

At Bhimkali Temple, Himachal Pradesh

On 31st July our first stop was nearly 40 Kms at Bhimakali Temple in Sarahan. We could not curb our temptation to have fresh apples, so we ate fresh juicy apples. Of course, the apples needed some more sunshine to get sweetness. The aroma of course was natural. We came across scores of orchards fully laden with fruits. Apart from apples, there were pears and Chuli (a fruit close to an apricot but smaller in size and sour in taste).

We arrived at Bhimakali Temple. The deity is Kuldevi (Family Deity) of Raja Vir Bhadra Singh's family, who also had his private helipad close by. The temple trust looks after the 700-year-old temple. It was renovated by Raja Vir Bhadra Singh's family from time to time. It has huge complex and I saw very majestic, framed pictures of temple complex during the winter with snow covered hills around. Close to the temple there were several shops selling Prasad and other offerings for the deity.

It was time now to offer our prayers to the deity, Bhimakali. After parking the car, we covered the ground close to the entrance, where after alighting 8-10 steps we removed our shoes and washed our hands. It was another 10-odd steps which took us to the compound, where we were asked to deposit all our electronic gadgetry (including cell phones). We were advised to cover our heads with coloured (red, yellow, etc.) caps. After covering a few more steps, we were at the base of the temple itself. We saw that all the doors were thick and covered with ornamentally carved silver. We could also see chains which earlier used to ring bells on top of the temple building. There were brass bells on each entrance and would give a good resonating sound. I am sure that the bells sound must be covering a good distance in that valley and must be giving some kind of divine feeling to those coming especially in winter when all around snow would have covered. In fact, I had seen a photograph in winter setting of the temple and in snow it was looking very majestic. Anyhow, after covering 3 floors of narrow, winding wooden stairs, we were at the feet of Bhimakali. We were told that during Navratri the temple is thronged with devotees. At this time, there were only a handful of us. The priest patiently narrated about various idols and also explained the daily rituals, which are performed dutifully. He also tied sacred thread and applied Tilak on our foreheads. He also gave us Prasad and Charanaamrit and when I recounted that in Amer (Jaipur), the priest gives local brew as a special Charana Amrit, he too gave us a spoonful of liquor to each of us and while doing so, he chanted Mantras. Perhaps, believing us to be true devotees he even gave each of us a packet of Dhoop/Essence. We were feeling elated and blessed. Normally, in temples Priests give hardly anytime to the individual devotees unless they are some VIPs. After bidding goodbye to the Priest, we returned and on reaching the place where we had deposited our electronics, we were allowed to take some snaps. After covering the same route, we put on our shoes and alighted car for onward march.

It is true that at each night shelter, we were required to bring all the baggage to our rooms and the next day take it back. However, I had enjoyed the privilege and courtesy of my mates in lifting baggage. It was their kindness but believe me it was not my arrogance but physical condition, which my mates understood well. In turn, I used to narrate anecdotes and my life experiences and as such our journey time would pass pleasantly in enjoying the trip.

From Bhimakali Temple in Sarahan we came back to Jeori on the main Road and started towards Sangla, nearly a hundred Kms from Sarahan. On way we took lunch at a wayside Dhaba. The vegetarian food, consisting of good quality Basmati Rice, Rajma and Himachali Kadhi was excellent. The food was fresh but not spicy. I noticed another thing in HP that local Dhabas are particularly lenient about quantity of meals and do not at all haggle or charge extra for extra quantity of any item asked for by the customer. Generally, chutney and pickle are also placed along with freshly cut onions. I felt contented and welcome. The tea after meals was another plus as I am fussy about my teacup being filled with strong brew. It was a perfect match.

HP is called Dev Bhumi, like Kerala is called God's Own Land. The lush green trees, rivers, water bodies and hardworking people really make the place to be visited time and again. The scenic snow-capped mountains really attract and give a welcome call. It is not that there are no hardships for even where we were the height from sea level was well over 8000 to 10000 feet. HP has made good use of rivers by calling private companies to generate electricity by tapping water without making big dams or dislodging people. The Jaypee's had put up plants with a total capacity of 1000 Megawatts. After sustaining losseso, they sold the entire set up to JSW Energy, who are running plants successfully. There are dozens of even single digit MW plants. All this has made HP electricity surplus state and that too without wasting any water.

Glimpses of Dev Bhumi Himachal Pradesh, including Hidimba Temple, Manali

Similarly, BRO is doing excellent work in coordination with the State PWD for widening and making all weather roads. The climate is harsh. At some places melting and shifting glaciers pose problems. Cloud burst and following devastations make conditions really tough, but BRO is really doing a commendable job in making roads motorable. We could ourselves see roads having been blocked by landslides and BRO making alternate roads and bridges by diverting traffic but keeping in mind convenience and least hampering of traffic. We reached PWD Rest House around 5 p.m. and after depositing our baggage and having tea we came out to have a view of the local market. The Rest House boasted some good fruit trees and wines. It is a small town, but most of the utilities were available. The Evening ritual of 60 ml was repeated over freshly prepared chicken and fish. The Quilt made the sleep comfortable for over 10000' it had become cold even during the summer. Dreaming of another day of adventure, the night passed peacefully.

Satisfaction Demonstrable on visiting Chitkul

In front of Kibber Village in Himachal Pradesh (Lahul/Spiti)

 As the page of the calendar changed from July to August, so had we changed the terrain of our travel from lush green tall pine and other trees covering the mountains, the trees started thinning out. Instead of Sutlej now we had the company of Baspa River. The mountainous range varied in color and even its very structure, somewhere it would be just like soil like earth, somewhere concrete and somewhere solid rocks. The colors would be amazing and ever-changing. We could see limestone and gravel of different grades. BRO gets plenty of raw material from the site itself. We had seen calibrated blasts, completely controlled drilling with a remote, carried on robot like vans manipulated by trained engineers. One would definitely be impressed by imbibing modern techniques and automation to speed up work so that there was the least possible hampering of traffic.

On August 1, our first destination was Chitkul via Raksham, a distance of around 25 Kms. Chitkul is the last habitable village on the Indo-Tibetan border, which is another 100 Kms from there. The road was mountainous and on the way we could see devastation made by cloud burst just a week ago. It washed away stones, boulders and trees. The work was still going on to make the road safe from falling rocks. Landslides are common and intermittently we could find signs. Of course, towards river side there were pine trees and apple orchards. We could also see agricultural crops like potatoes, peas, some varieties of greens having been sown. We could see the efforts of the Forest Department in planting new trees. The village Raksham on way has won a national prize for being ideal clean village. I noticed that Village Panchayats are doing wonderful work in preserving environment and they enforce and invoke their authority in the interest of safeguarding environment, like not allowing camping too close to water bodies and ensuring waste is not left behind. Once again, we were requested by a passerby to handover the keys of his shop in Chitkul's Bawa Dhaba as by mistake he had brought with him keys of the shop. We of course obliged him and marvelled over the trust he had deposed in strangers for he himself could have delivered the key but in a way showed to us that he too can be trusted with any such request. We also saw a board on a wayside Dhaba in Chitkul claiming as the last Dhaba of India, but it was not so as there were a couple of more beyond that point. In fact, we found one, named Last Destination, more than a 1 Km away from the village when we proceeded further to see the first post of ITBP beyond which entry was restricted. When we enquired Mr. Negi about Last Destination, he told us that for a single room he charges 2 to 3 thousand Rupees per night. This place was earlier frequented by traders from across the border. Here we were at a height of 11300' and thinning of oxygen was noticeable. We could also find some temporary camping sites on way back. Of course, on way back we took freshly prepared Vegetable Momos with hot chili sauce and tea at Bawa's Dhaba but ensured payment of the bill, which was reasonable, and we had the satisfaction of having enjoyed a meal in the last (or first) habitable village on this side of India.

During trip to Himachal Pradesh, I must compliment that there was awareness about cleanliness and even at remote places sweeping of roads was being carried out. Markets and roads were also clean and above all, our temples were also clean. It was really heartening to note. I also witnessed notices, near springs that in Himachal there was no need to buy bottled water, as the water from natural bodies was safe for drinking. Being curious about the prices of various produces, especially apples, when enquired we were told that in Upper Kinnaur generally a carton contains around 10-12 Kgs apples and that in lower Kinnaur contains double the weight. In upper Kinnaur the size of apples is somewhat smaller, but apples contain a lot of aroma, and as such these apples are much in demand. In upper Kinnaur apples will start coming in the market after mid-September and by that time pine-nuts would also be ready. Rajma would have another product available there. An apple carton was going for around Rs. 3000/-. Trucks take around 24 hours to reach Delhi. Plucking of apples was so done as to cover the handling and journey period up to end-user. Pears, apricots, peaches, plums had started pouring in for auction in markets. Pears go cheaper for requiring tender handling and shorter shelf-life. A bag of 50 Kgs of fresh peas would fetch around Rs. 3500/-. We tried some fresh peas; they were really tender and sweet. From orchards or farms the produces are brought by labourer on their backs in bags/baskets. On our return journey from Chitkul, we stopped for a while at the village of Raksham, which has won a national prize for being an ideal village and we took some snaps. Snaps of course, were taken at other scenic spots on the way back to Sangla. The previous day, in Sangla, we also picked some fresh fruits, biscuits and other munchies. We also tried some sweets as cravings for sweets were on the rise.

Our night shelter that day was Rekong Peo, the district Headquarters of Kalpa. The distance from Sangla was around 41 km. by mountainous road, where widening of roads or repairs were almost an unending exercise. In fact, we too had to stop for almost an hour after blasting had been done and debris was being collected. One could only marvel at how precisely the mountains are cut so as not to leave loose stones endangering passersby. Man's continuing endeavour to win over nature despite facing continuing failures and hardships.

By the way, I would like to tell my readers that whenever and whatever I write, I see to it that what I write is unbiased and objective. I highlight points which deserve to be mentioned or that have attracted my attention, which I honestly share. Before entering Rekong Peo Rest House, we thought it advisable to have a late lunch of Himachali dishes in a roadside Dhaba. The food was simple but filling.

After arriving at the Rest House, we settled down and were served tea. After a while, we sat down for our sundowner, and around nine in the evening, we had our dinner in the dining room. Simple but delicious vegetarian meal and retired for the night with assurance to be served our tea around 7 in the morning, so that by Nine we could start our day's journey after breakfast. The following day, we were to first cover Kalpa, around 5 Kms. as we learned that from there, on a clear day, one can see formation of 7 to 8' high ice Shivlinga. There is az a Devi Temple . Here, the foreigners also get interline permit to enter Lahaul-Spiti.

On 2nd August, we started as planned but being foggy on the hill we could hardly see the formation of Shivalinga, but our driver did show us a picture of the same, which he had taken on an earlier visit. It was really spectacular.

550 year old Mummy at Giu

I have Resolved NOT to Stop

In Kalpa, we also saw raw pine nuts, which would be ready by following month only. We descended and came on the main road for our day's destination, Tabo via Nako and Giu. The journey was supposed to be long in hilly tract. At times, we would be on the left side of the road and a little later on the right side. The landscape kept us mesmerized. There was hardly any patch which was not being under widening or repair. Rivers were changing but at no point we were without any water bodies. We had entered the Spiti area. It was dry. The climb was increasing. As a daily ritual, we used to take tablet after breakfast to keep our lungs functioning even with less oxygen and also by now, we had somewhat got acclimatized. We saw that the Police there was vigilant and having noticed our driver without dress, he had to shell out Rs. 100/- as Challan. Perhaps, strict adherence of traffic rules was also needed for terrain . We l l turned onto a side road to go to Giu, which has a more than 550 years old mummy. From road the distance is around 11 Kms. We were wonder struck to find mummy's shining teeth and hair. The mummy of Lama in some Yogic posture was carbon-dated to find exact age. We were told that during summer almost 100 cars come daily. At a time 7 persons are allowed entry into a tiny room where the mummy was kept in a glass cage. A nice temple was under construction. We also had refreshing tea at the tea stall within the compound. Close to the track to this place also flows a pitch-dark black Nullah. We saw black earth on the side. Before the temple, there was a village and small boys waved at us to say welcome.

Close to 550-year Mummy in Giu (L to R) (Self, Driver Sunil and Pardeep)

Dev Bhumi, Himachal Pradesh at 76

People travelling on foot through the Gramphu-Batal-Kaza Road. Closed for 7 months and one of the toughest adventure roads on the planet. On that stretch of 80 kms there are no houses, no people and no vehicles to give way to. Some sections you need to cross before 1-2PM to avoid getting stuck in the rising flow of melting glacial water.

Before, coming to Giu, we had gone to see Nako Lake. By the time we reached there we were feeling hungry, and we thought it advisable to have simple meals in a Kangri Dhaba. The owner served the meal with smile on his face and made us feel welcome. He was a jovial fellow and guided us to the lake. However, the road was blocked as it was under construction. We had to come back a Km to find another route through a local village leading to the lake. Surprisingly, geographically, it was part of Kinnaur district. There is a monastery also. The lake provides a good source of water to the villagers, who now have apple orchards apart from cultivation of potatoes, peas etc. There are around 150 steps down from where the car can be parked. The blue lake was beautiful. I had seen an orange-coloured shrub near Kangri Dhaba and out of curiosity asked about it. I was told that it is called Som Lata and it has potential medicinal values, especially for the treatment of Asthma. I had read somewhere that Aryans used to have Som Ras, which was extracted from some shrub. I wonder if it has any connection. Also, intriguing was the word Lata meaning creeper, whereas it was just a shrub. I had also read that Lokmanya Tilak believed Aryans to be part of the Himalayas, based on his findings of shrubs used by the

I have Resolved NOT to Stop

locals. I cannot subscribe to any theory but cannot resist mentioning what I recall on having seen Som Lata. We also found plenty of rose bush. Apart from, bushes, we could also find many types of birds. The most common was crow (raven black). Himachal Pradesh is known for Wetland Birds, apart from Birds of Prey and both ground and aerial feeding birds and of course arboreal birds. There are migratory birds also. We could see a number of species of birds flying, hopping and swimming.

By the time we reached Kaza, it was quite late. We were lucky to find a place in the Rest House but we had to order meal from outside. We are not sure whether it was there custom to mix chicken and lamb or not but that was the mixed dish, which we were served or it could have been the portions left were mixed to fulfil our order. Otherwise, the other dishes and Chapatis were tasty. The food was enjoyable after long journey and of course after our evening venture for a cocktail. We hit the bed to be woken up next morning with refreshing tea.

Grapes at an elevation of 3745m above sea level. This is from the vineyard of the family where we bought the angoori.

Yes, of course, I almost forgot to mention an incident, which was really a highpoint of our adventurous tour. Having heard about the local brew, Angoori in Kinnaur, we searched for it and could not get

Dev Bhumi, Himachal Pradesh at 76

any clue. Then someone suggested that there will be a village Ribba on our way, where we would be able to find, what we were searching for. We were also told that it was on the main road itself and it would not require any lengthy and time-consuming detours. Right, he was, and on the way, we did find village Ribba. When we started asking people walking around or even the shopkeepers, we were told to enquire in the village and perhaps the Rest House people will be able to guide us. It was a 1 Km drive to the village, and we enquired a number of persons, who told us yes it would be available somewhere, but no one would guide us to the right spot. We even found a couple of people (including ladies) carrying bottles, but all of them said that they were going to offer this to Devta and that we should go further. It was almost getting frustrating and seemed like a waste of time, when we noticed a couple of guys, who appeared high. When we asked them, first they would tell us yes someone in the village must have it but not tell us as to who he would be. When we enquired as to what generally, the price was one of them mentioned atrocious price of around Ra. 3000 per bottle. We had almost given up, when one of them came to our rescue and said that we will have to go back on the main road for half a mile where we would find a road leading to a compound and that there was Dada ji or Baba ji whose family brews Angoori for the past 200 years and that is where we would find good quality Angoori of our choice. Although, we had become frustrated, we thought of giving it one last try, and believe me, close to the bridge described by them, we could find a motorable pathway leading to a compound. At the gate, we found a couple of young boys, who opened the gate and after covering another 200 yards through apple orchards and grape vines, we found a huge house. There was no one to be seen. No bell was visible. A door and steps were leading to the upper Storey. When two of us went close to the upper Storey a dog had started barking (thank God did not come out charging) and lady of the house came out and on being enquired about confirmed in the affirmative about the availability of Angoori. On being enquired she mentioned that a Gallon of it was for 4000/- and a Litre for Rs, 1000/- and a bottle for Rs. 800/-. Since we had made up our minds to try it, we asked for a bottle. Believe me, the lady said, bring the bottle, for which we emptied one of the water bottles and got the much-expected Angoori. We also took a fresh apple each from the tree and enjoyed it. So that evening we tried Angoori (not cocktail, which was postponed for the following night). It was quite potent for which we were forewarned. Diluted with water it almost tasted like grape juice and believe me all of us enjoyed it thoroughly. There was no hangover, no nasal congestion, andconstipation and it turned out to be a good excuse in venturing on this adventure. We could sleep soundly. Of course, we had taken care to restrict the quantity to be taken. It was gem of a discovery and fulfilment of taste buds longing for something new and unique.

View of Dhankar Monastry on the way to Kibber Village

Kee Gompa

Some of you must find the story of Ribba, rib-tickling where we were in search of something like rabid dogs in search of water. We could have very easily abandoned the search, but perhaps that would have made our effort seem half-hearted and like we had lost our adventure. It was not for nothing that there were a couple of buses arriving daily from distant places.

In Spiti, most of the residents are Buddhists, and we could see flags with Mani Mantras adorning various places. We had seen Yaks and cows, mules and goats and sheep. Goats we could see climbed steep hills easily. Spiti, is known for its snow Leopard, who among other things, eat Marcarian shrubs. Ibex and Bharal, besides the fox are other animals. To view Snow Leopard, people are ready to pay any amount.

At the Entrance of Tabo Monastery

On Angoori of Ribba, a friend from Himachal had mentioned that he had not heard of this brew, but believe me it was not imaginary, and indeed, it does exist. Many of us might not have heard of Kaisar-Kasturi in Rajasthan but it does exist and was very much liked even by royal families. At times, such brews remain hidden from wider knowledge or remain popular among limited communities or area.

On 3rd August, 2019, as per our original plan, after breakfast we headed for Tabo Monastery. It is almost a millennium old. After taking off our shoes and having deposited our electronic gadgets we were allowed to enter the Monastery's main hall, where there were impressive Lord Buddha's statues and the Head Priest with the help of a hand-held lamp showed us around. We were wonder struck to see wall paintings depicting various facets of Lord Buddha's life. The painting had faded but only a little and one could easily see vivacity. A foreign lady was in deep meditation in the hall. The Monastery sells wall hangings and other artifacts. We placed some donation and also offered our prayers. Once we were out of compound of the Monastery, we noticed some shops selling artefacts and jewellery. As I am a compulsive buyer, I settled for a Turquoise Necklace for my elder daughter. After haggling for price, we struck a bargain deal for Rs. 1500/- for two necklaces, as against originally asked price of Rs. 1100/- each.

I have Resolved NOT to Stop

Lunch we had in a Restaurant, and changed dishes also. After which headed for Kibber Village, which heretofore was the highest motorable village in Asia. The place of pride now is with Komic. We saw herds of blue sheep and were amazed to see goats grazing on top of steep hills. The village is around 20 Kms from Kaza, our night shelter. Shila peak was visible. We reached Kibber, where our car was parked, and one could see village perched on a hill and fields of potatoes and peas were making it a perfect place to live. In hills different owners make boundaries of their fields with stones and from a distance, they really present some kind of design as some take the form of heart. The village was known for sighting of snow leopards during November/December. They even eat Myricaria shrubs. There are 400 plants species and many of them have medicinal or spicy properties. These are collected by local village doctor, known as Amchis. On way back we also stopped at the famous Kee Gompa. The Lamas is known for the Chham dance and Buchen dance.

The view of Spiti valley on the way to Kibber village near Kaza.

We arrived at Kaza Market, and where we got our car filled with petrol and incidentally, it was supposedly the highest petrol station (Indian Oil). Kaza also boasts of the highest Polling Station. We felt elated and privileged to have had the lifetime chance to visit these places. We could not curb our temptation to try fresh Jalebis and hot Pakoras. If eyes could get what they were looking for, how could our pallet lag behind. As the next morning we were to start by 0630 we made preparations accordingly. The whole evening and night we had to spend without light but that did not bother us much, as we were ready for our candlelight dinner after our appetizer of a cocktail savoured by all of us.

The original plan for 4th August was to camp near Chandratal Lake in a Tent. We were advised against this as at our advanced age, the risk was too high, as lack of oxygen could have posed a problem. Also recently, The Village Panchayat made it compulsory to camp at least a Km away from the lake. We could see dozens and dozens of such camps. As we were supposed to cross two high passes, first the Kunzam Pass (4551 meters) and then the Rohtang pass (3978 meters) and also cover Chandratal, we started early from Kaza around as scheduled by 06:30 hrs. These passes remain open for a limited period of the year and are quite treacherous both for terrain and slippery stones caused by melting glaciers. We had made up our mind to have breakfast on way. The landscape was ever changing. Every curve would change the colour. The roads were again being widened. The sky was a clear blue, and we could see clearly for miles. The snow-clad peaks appeared so close as we could touch them with hand. The river flowing down was breath-taking.

At the entrance of Chandratal   *At Rohtang Pass*

At Losar, we had breakfast and could see plenty of yaks and cows. From Losar after covering 19 Kms we came at entry point of Kunzam Pass. All motorists are supposed to take a Parikrama of a place meant to be prayed and revered. We too followed the custom so as to invoke good luck during journey. A coin is also pasted and if it remains stuck, the remaining journey was supposedly going to be safe. Though we are not orthodox, we do not like to disobey a custom and hurt feelings of others.

Sunrise at Losar (4090m) with Mountains and Farms

Apart from motorists, we also came across pedestrian passers-by, reminding us of olden times. After covering another 14 Kms. we took a turn to go to Chandratal Lake, which is 23 Kms from that point and at the height of 13300' it is nature's gift to mankind. It remains frozen during winter. As per Hindu Mythology, it was here that Lord Indra 's Chariot was supposed to have taken, the eldest Pandava, Yudhistra to Heaven in Mortal Form. It was one Km on foot from the allowed parking area as after that a stone wall stalls further drive. Covering 23 Kms distance back, we were again on our way to Rohtang Pass and for which we had yet to cover many hurdles.

Having seen pedestrians crossing Kunzam Pass, I recall having seen an advertisement at Kangra Dhaba offering a 40-day trip to Nepal and Bhutan entailing hiking also. In earlier times, it was a common practice that traders would come from across the border to exchange goods through barter system. Each one used to find items of one's necessity. At places BRO teams were working to make travel hassle-free despite odds against them. They really do commendable job sustaining hardships of rough and tough weather and terrain. We had covered a good part of Spiti and Lahaul that we started facing melting glaciers' water coming down in nullahs. Some of them were easily manageable and some did create difficulty. We were lucky enough to cross over a dozen of big and

Dev Bhumi, Himachal Pradesh at 76

small nullahs. We used to enquire from oncoming traffic, even on motorbikes, as to how was rest of the journey. We were in a way forewarned that two of them were really nasty. They were wide enough and slippery stones make Tyres stuck in stones. Then they will merely whirl and swirl but would not make forward or backward movement. Placing and removing stones in ice cold water was yet another problem. One of them was known as Pagla Nullah, which reminded me similarly named Nullah in Ladakh passes. We had almost come towards the end of lines of such Nullahs that we really got caught in Pagla Nullah. Our efforts did not succeed. Then luckily, we found one long wire and Pradeep persuaded with monetary reward to one of the four-wheel drivers to tie up wire and give our car a push forward, while 7-8 persons would shake up the car. Reluctantly he agreed and we were able to move a couple of feet forward and once the wire was removed, we got stuck again. It was only God's intervention that the driver agreed to repeat the act of pulling our vehicle and thanks God we were once again on plain road. It took almost 90 grilling minutes. If we would not have been saved, perhaps, we would have sought a lift and abandoned the car for the night stay. This would have been fatal, and with every passing minute the water was increasing, and we would have been in really deep trouble. We were yet to cross a couple of more but slightly less deadly nullahs and luckily thereafter we could surmount every problem.

Grueling Experience in Icy Cold Glacier Water (which forms Chandra River and Merges with Chenab) when our Car got Stuck at Pagla Nalah, Near Gramphu-Batal

I have Resolved NOT to Stop

Having crossed Kunzam Pass, we entered Rohtang Pass, luckily there was a little drizzle, but the sky was covered with fog. There was heavy traffic due to road diversion. We safely reached Point Zero of Rohtang Pass. Thereafter, we had to slow down due to fog and heavy traffic, but we reached Manali without any problem and checked into the new Forest Guest House, which was comfortable, cozy and appeared heavenly place welcoming and comforting us after the ordeal of the day. That was perhaps the Climax of our journey, and it gave us sane advice that on such terrain depend upon a dependable four-wheel drive instead of looking for comfort of Toyota Innova.

Thanks friends, I feel satisfied and it encourages me to go on writing further about my visit to Kinnaur and Lahaul/Spiti. I must also mention that rivers from those areas come to Punjab and that apart from Sutlej, Vyas River has tributaries from rivers there. Rivers like Baspa and Spiti and a couple of more of them make important contribution in development. Bhakra and Pong dams are good examples of such contributions. A canal from Vyas also takes water to Bhakra, while controlling water-level there. I must also mention of 2.9 Km long Atal Tunnel which connects Kiratpur-Manali to eastern Pir Panjal range. which will make travel much easier. Another 8.8 Km long tunnel connecting the Manali-Leh section of Rohtang Pass was under advance stage of completion. In Pir Panjal Mountain Range it would be world's highest tunnel and reduce distance by as many as 46 Kms besides providing round the year travel.

Manali was lush green as ever. On the way we had also seen a number of motor cyclists going to Mani Karan like Kanwarias, who go to Ganges to fetch water during the month of Shravana. It was just 23 Km and we had half a mind to go there but the day had really been long and tiring so we left it for the next time. After evening celebration with nice shots of whisky and good food, we rightly deserved night rest. The following day, after breakfast and having checked out went to see famous Hidimba Temple. It is said that she had done Tapasya in that very cave. We could also see some figure on the rock, which are said to be those of Hidimba. She is revered there, and people throng the temple and there is an annual ritual also.

Dev Bhumi, Himachal Pradesh at 76

Again, I could not resist making purchases of some shawls and walnuts of HP. Walnuts were really hard. Shawls were for gifting away. We also saw Russian Painter, Fredrick Roerich's estate. He had married to Devika Rani, Dada Saheb Phalke Award winner and Diya of Bollywood in her time and with her ex-husband, Himanshu Rai had produced films in famous Bombay Talkies. She is also credited to have introduced Ashok Kumar to films. It is a huge estate. We were then on our way to Mandi through scenic hilly road and in between we enjoyed natural beauty and fresh air. Pradeep had lined up Guest House in Mandi through courtesy of his dear friend the Doctor-Director of Medical College there and evening we were entertained at a Restaurant where his Excise Commissioner friend, Pritpal Singh, who too hailed from Bilaspur like himself also gave us company. It was very lavish dinner and of course evening could not have gone without proper appetizer. We really enjoyed that evening chatting. During the course of conversation, I learnt that the Ruler of Bilaspur had joined India much after merger of even Junagarh and Hyderabad. At least I was not aware of this historical fact till then.

Next day, by 1 PM we reached Pradeep's place in Chandigarh, having stopped on the way for our breakfast near River Bias. To make the trip even sweeter, I even bought a large bottle of fresh honey from roadside honeybee keeper. Sweet memories linger on, over a spoon of honey and my corn flakes taste much sweeter to think of the trip.

I have attempted to share some photographs of my trip to Himachal Pradesh (Kinnaur and Lahul/Spiti). I had penned my journey, and believe me, the places are really amazing and worth visiting. Words cannot describe the thrill one gets while there. I might have missed mangoes during that period, but I had much more to enjoy. I am fully in support of our PM's advice that we should visit every nook and corner of our country, which is amazing. When I was in Spain, I learned that the country gets double the number of tourists than its population. I used to marvel and try to find reasons. One word which always cropped up was "courtesy", which encompasses many more traits which attract tourists. It is not that India lacks nature's beauty and architectural heritage, besides many other things, like, music, dances and cuisines. In fact, there is plenty of it. Infrastructure, banking etc are also being taken care of. Perhaps, there is need to be more aggressive in our campaigning and presenting every bit with a bit of national pride. Hospitable we are. We have various recipes to please any palette and present an eye-catching platter. There is perhaps really need to brand our tourism and market it properly, in a composite manner with much more vigor and extensive publicity. Not only more such visits would mean entertainment or religious quenching, increasing knowledge, employment but also physical fitness. Once we have increased fervor to go on such tours, like we go on pilgrimages, it can turn into a weekly affair, as in the West, where weekend is spent on beaches, seashores or some place to relax and rejuvenate for the next week. During my service, I have seen many such places and have mostly found that India has much more to offer. There is need to exploit the full potential. I sincerely wish that there would be no delay to show the needed will for required aggression.

I may add that in February 2023 I attended in Chandigarh the marriage of Chandan s/o dear Pardeep Gupta and what a change I found in the young lad turning into a somewhat bulky and bearded Chandan. Of course, I also took the opportunity to strike my Bucket's List of rediscovering the Toy Train from Kalka to Shimla, which passes through numerous tunnels and Tunnel No. 33 is longest being 1579 Meters long and at a height of 5118'. It is really an engineering marvel being one of the oldest hill tracks, but the pity is that it is no longer pulled by Steam Engine but by Diesel Engine. However, the journey is most enjoyable as one passes through trees, and brooks and at times one is able to see down below vehicular traffic and of course, towns and settlements. Barog is the most beautiful station, and the halt is also for a little longer, which makes people to add to their adventure by having hot tea/coffee and snacks. Eagerness to go on and on never stops but at least one can always give oneself a pause but not for long and longing for searching for new venture should never end. So be it!

Glimpses of Buntings

Roadside Shrines

Roadside slogans

I have Resolved NOT to Stop

Divya enroute Leh, mighty mountains in the background

6th chapter

Revisit of Ladakh and Kayakalp at 76

Lure of Ladakh was not imaginary

The charm of Ladakh got rekindled once my daughter, Divya on her visit from Detroit (USA) wished that she was keen to visit Ladakh and if possible, a short spell at Kayakalp in Palampur. I jumped over the idea and immediately got bookings for both of us for Ladakh (Leh) in September 2019. The idea was not only to visit some of the places, which I had gone earlier but also add a few more places, especially, as my nephew, Gorav himself, was going to be present in Ladakh, and naturally, his help would be immense.

Once at the Leh Airport and before being received by my nephew Gorav, to our surprise, the young and dynamic Member of Parliament, Jamyang Tsering Namgyal was met at the airport. There were also quite a few Ladakhi men and women in traditional ornamental dresses carrying Kalash (Water Vessels), understandably carrying water from Kanyakumari for merging in the Indus River; an emotional nationalistic scene and feel. These efforts I shall mention a little later. Ladakh is geographically the largest Parliamentary seat.

Having had Lunch and rested, Divya took the advice of seeing the Shanti Stupa and War Memorial. It turned out to be a wise decision, as due to the visit of GOC Northern Command, there was also a well-presented cultural programme at the War Memorial. She felt emotionally moved and appreciated well-crafted and heart-touching performances. On our return and after we had freshened up, it was time for an elaborate, well-laid dinner. Naturally, day's toil and full belly made us want to have sound sleep.

Divya at Leh

Divya at war memorial in Leh attending cultural performances

The next day, we were to start at 9 a.m. after breakfast. We also had a packed lunch and plenty of juices and tepid warm water for the journey, for the aim was to go to Drass, the actual war theatre of Kargil, where a Memorial has been built to honour Kargil Heroes. It was also decided that on the way to Drass we would not stop at spots, like Confluence of the Indus and Zanskar to be must see places, to save time for covering the long journey and as that could be done the following day, while returning. On the way there were several restaurants and surprisingly, many of them named themselves Punjabi Dhabas, whereas the matter of fact is that they hardly sell anything even remotely connected with Punjabi dishes. Yes, one can get Noodles, Thupka, Momos and Rice to be topped up with Ladakhi tea. A few of course, sell Delhi-type boiled tea. However, we made an exception by taking a couple of snaps at the confluence of the River Indus and River Zanskar but only from the top road side. The roads were curvaceous but well carpeted and smooth, except at one or two places. The scenic beauty was beyond description. Vegetation was also minimal. Every hill or hillock presented a different picture. Some were bare earth with a few shrubs, some with grass, some were solid rocks, from jet black to white. At many places one could get the feel as if painting had been done on rocks. At places, one could find flowing water having made structures. It is not at all easy to describe the pleasure one gets when one's eyes are on them.

Divya enjoying Chilly Morning at Kargil Night Shelter

The distance which we were to cover that day from Leh to go to Drass, where there is the Kargil War Memorial and broadly the war theatre was 325 Kms, as first even by-passing the town of Kargil we had to come back 62 Kms. for a night's stay. As I had mentioned earlier, we had decided not to stop while our outward journey was in progress and do so only during our inward journey, with the aim of being able to see the War Memorial with the peace and patience it deserves. It could not be touched and come back after merely performing a ritual. We were joined, for the trip by Mr. Jagdish and his wife Sudesh, whom Gorav had introduced the previous night, over dinner, as his senior colleagues. They proved to be a lively company and Jagdish was always there to extend his helping hand to me and I got the privilege of always occupying the front seat, for it was easier to mount a four-wheeler. We started, as planned, around 9.30 a.m. after a sumptuous breakfast, and on top of that, we also carried a packed lunch and enough drinks and water. I realized on my earlier trip in 2018 that though there are a number of Dhabas/Restaurants all of them virtually serve local food only. Tea also one may not get to one's taste, but I was told that Ladakhi tea with salted butter was in fact better to withstand a lack of Oxygen.

Although I knew from my earlier trip that my prepaid Airtel phone would not work because of a networking problem, I still carried it and found a solution in Jio Wi-Fi, which had much better network coverage. I may also add and impress upon you that life was going on normally and there were no unnecessary roadblocks after revocation of Article 370. There were ample examples, to conclude that disturbance of any kind was not noticeable and that there was a need to quell the designs of rumour mongers and also encourage more people to visit both the union territories. This will also support locals economically and normal sustenance and of course much needed development.

We had taken NH-1 and I felt overwhelmed and elated, as also moments of pride came in my mind, somewhat similarly, when I had covered NH-1 from Key West in the US. Here road goes to Srinagar and is one of the best all weather, fully carpeted tarmac road. We found that we were traveling generally at a height of 10-11,000' but at places it was over 13000'. Such places are windy and chilly and it almost makes me shiver to even think of it. The road was obviously curvaceous and there were sharp curves and bends, and at some places there were almost blind spots. To begin with, plantation was scanty and as one progressed one could find an increasing number of trees. Each hill had a different formation and mostly loose earth mounds. The colours and sizes of each mound were also different, from jet black to grey, brown, stony and some were with small bushes or some grass. Perhaps, there is need to develop forestry much faster to save soil erosion, which causes floods and falling debris even choke whatever drainage was there during the rainy season, even though scanty. Indus River flows on the left side of the road and for me it was one of the high points of our journey, and I always got overwhelmed whenever I was able to see it flowing. It really charmed me like anything, and I got mesmerized.

Hills on the way from Leh to Kargil

I very well know it becomes totally drab as a narration without photographs. My apologies for that, as I am not at all a good camera handler and I await the snaps taken by others, like my daughter. Nevertheless, I shall do whatever was possible. For the time being, let me continue with my efforts to make the journey as pleasing as it could be in words. As I had mentioned the greenery on the roadside was on the increase. One could also see some farming in valley down below. The region boasts rivers. There is the Dras River, which originates in Macloi Glacier, and the river itself is just about 68 Kms. long. The Suru River is also a tributary to Indus and it in turn gets its tributes from Karaste River. That makes valley rich and fertile and the Kargil area is known for finest quality of apricots. Oil is also extracted from its seeds, which is supposedly good for joint pains. Dry apricots are also used in some dishes. Kargil is a reasonably large town. In fact, the road to Drass passes through market, which was abuzz with activities. One could also see well-dressed happy children returning from school in

I have Resolved NOT to Stop

their school uniforms. It took us nearly half an hour to cross the market. Normal activities on roads and markets were another proof of normalcy in the region and indeed a slap on the face of rumour mongers. There were a lot of vehicles at roadside workshops for repairs. It appears that Kargil has good mechanics and workshops. Timber also serves as another flourishing trade in the region.

At Kargil War Memorial with Naik Sunil Sharma

We reached Drass and were impressed to see the War Memorial, well laid out and kept. The location could not be better. Right behind were all the hilltops, like Tololing, Rhino. Batra Top and Tiger Hills, commonly known names associated with the Kargil War. There were wheelchairs for those needing such an assistance. Naik Sunil Sharma gave a vivid description of the happenings during the Kargil War. The red-stone statues of war heroes were there. A number of Param Vir Chakras, Mahavir Chakras and Veer Chakras were awarded. The Pakistani treachery of breaching the agreement by vacating posts during the winter season was given a befitting reply. It also gave us a lesson as not to ever trust any rogue neighbour, who has no decency to keep a word. We need to be a little extra cautious. Daily violations of cross border firing even on civilians cannot be overlooked. There was also a video show. We enjoyed a warm cup of tea much needed on somewhat cold evening. The washrooms were clean and well kept. A small donation of Rs. 5/- had been suggested, which I was too happy to donate, in fact, in multiples. I had seen a similar notice at the famous Wangchuk School of 3 Idiots fame. We were filled with pride, and our heads bowed to those who had given their lives for our safe future. In fact, the narration of Naik Sunil Sharma started with "Shahidon ki Chitaon par Lagange Har Baras Mele, Watan Par Mitne Walon ka Yahi Baki Nishan Hoga', which aptly appeared emotional but rather a reality. It was satisfaction enough to have paid reverence at the Memorial.

We returned to Kargil for our night stay. After welcome hot tea and snacks, we freshened up to have dinner, which I and my daughter skipped, and we were constrained to take soup only for we felt that we were emotionally full and wanted to retire early for the night and be fresh for journey back on the next day. The next day we decided to start after breakfast with packed lunch around 0830 hrs. The day was a memorable one and we felt that at least we were able to walk, where our heroes had run one after the other in a hurry to lay down their lives for our safety and security.

Beautiful morning view at Kargil

After sound sleep, we woke up fresh on the morning of September 18, and freshly brewed tea was immediately brought. In somewhat cold morning tea was really refreshing. For breakfast we were ready on time. Tasty food made the mood to march for a supposedly hectic day ahead. As a second thought, a Medical Attendant was called to check

I have Resolved NOT to Stop

our BP and other significant parameters. I was found with low BP and Sudesh were found to have less Oxygen (under 90). So, we decided to check with the doctor, especially as the following day we had planned to go to Pangong Lake, passing through over 17,500' Chang La.

In the MI Room, the attendants promptly rechecked and confirmed earlier findings. We were assured prompt consultation with the doctor as soon as he finished with the on-going patient. It is important to mention here that we saw two local ladies being administered oxygen and liquid through IVs. Two more local patients came, one was a girl student complaining of dizziness and nausea, and another was a boy also complaining of severe headache. They were immediately attended. to. Our Jawans are doing yeoman's job and the locals come seeking help without any kind of fear. After we were checked by the doctor and after he had advised medication and a line of treatment, like 20 minutes each of oxygen for both of us, we were again checked by the doctor for final advice. In his earnest opinion, he told us that it would be best to postponed, if possible, we planned trip of the next day but we went ahead as planned by taking the precaution of carrying personal oxygen cylinders with us. It was also discovered that I had not taken my daily medication for BP that morning. In any case, we were much relieved to find only minor problems, which could be easily taken care of. While we were going out, we found another local boy coming limping having met with an accident. It all showed that the local people trust our forces and were being served well and thereby commanding respect and people deposing trust in them. After thanking we rode the vehicle to embark on another fascinating day's adventure. I must also mention that the complex was sparklingly neat and clean and boasted a good number of flowers, mostly Sunflowers, looking fresh and healthy.

Once we came on the main road, we were once again on NH-1. On way back, we stopped at a Gompa, which I had noticed as it had huge Buddha carved out of rock on the main building. Later on, we discovered that it was more than a thousand years old Gompa. The Head Lama explained about various artifacts there. Close by was a Muslim shrine and I saw people paying their respects there by stopping their vehicles.

Visit of Gompa where a large Buddha was carved out of rock

We found at several places sign boards declaring, "Don't be Gama in the land of Lama". Gama was a famous wrestler of his time hailing from J&K. This was to caution candidly that though the roads are good, there is need for precaution and one must have patience, while driving at high speed. As they say Tranquilo in Spanish. In Hindi also we say, Sahaj Pake so Mitha Hoye. There is wisdom in the saying as over-speeding could be dangerous for self and others. So, Gama the famous wrestler with his known skills and speed to defeat his challenger need not be ideal on road but a Lama with Patience.

We stopped at the two high points, namely Namikala and Fatula. Both were chilly but presented an awesome view of the valley. We also made good use of our packed lunch, and in one of the officers' mess, we relished it with fresh tea of the type we like.

I have Resolved NOT to Stop

At Fatula Top – 13479 ft Altitude

Our next stop was near the confluence, where we could touch water of both the rivers. It is really very serene over there. It gives me a peaceful feeling. My daughter placed 5 stones in memory of her Mother (late Tripta), as is done by Buddhists in the memory of someone dear but having had departed from the world. At least, I could spend not only hours but perhaps days to experience such a peaceful and place of tranquility. Some may agree with me. Gorav told me that it was their favourite picnic spot where he usually brings all the paraphernalia and a cook for preparing fresh meal after the dip. Really a soulful experience.

Divya Near the Indus/Zanskar Confluence - Ready to place 5 stones in Memory of Tripta Bajaj (Mother)

Next stop was the world-famous Magnetic Valley. We could see the cars stopped in neutral taking automatic climb. A natural marvel. There were desert bikes available on rent for Rs. 1000/-. We of course were content with our own car taking upward climb without any difficulty.

How could we miss out on Pathar Saheb Gurudwara, where Guru Nanak Dev Ji's divine powers stopped the huge stone boulder throne by a villainous character from top of the hill? There is another Gurudwara in Leh city, where Guru Nanak Dev Ji is supposed to have deposited his Datun (dental brush) and on my earlier trip I had seen a huge tree standing there. Night shelter awaited our arrival with fresh tea, dinner, and a cozy bed to rest for an early start the following day.

Divya at Gurudwara Shri Pathar Saheb

Some words are easy to remember, and more so when, the word can be used in many ways, e.g. I learned the word 'Jullay' in Ladakhi means not only Hello but also Goodbye and Thanks. One word to tackle many situations. Another word commonly used is 'La' which means Land of High Pass and is suffixed with the name of the High Pass concerned. So far on our way from Kargil, we had passed Namki La (12,200') and Fotu La (13479'). Our next aim was to pass Chang La (over 17000') and eventually Khardung La (18,600' - Top of the world), the then highest motorable pass in the world. (I had earlier also done Nathu La in Sikkim).

I have Resolved NOT to Stop

So, we were all set to start with a packed lunch for our adventure with Changa La and Pangong Lake. Our apprehensions of having seen on TV a bit of a scuffle with Chinese intruding soldiers and their being pushed out, a day before the commencement of our journey from Delhi, were quelled and we were told that we were unlikely to encounter any hardship on that account. We also behaved like brave hearts and proceeded. The road up to a few Kms. of climb is fine, but after that patchy and not fully tarmacked as during winters roads tend to require extensive repairs. Melting glaciers and passing water flow make the journey slower. In any case caution is always better than speed. The view of valley and snow-capped mountains is amazing especially as blue sky adds to its charm. One can easily touch ice on the sides of the road. We could also see some yaks and other creatures on the way. Grazing animals looked somewhat smaller in size (even cows). Before heading towards Pangong Lake, we stopped to have lunch near a rivulet where arrangements for fresh tea was also made. It was a refreshing experience. The cracking bones could also get some rest. Our driver was also able to have the brakes fixed, which he thought were giving trouble, but it turned out that on height and hard braking had made the difference only in feel. With some rest, it was all fine to march on.

Divya with cousin, Gorav Bajaj at the Confluence.

After a drive of another two hours, we were at the beauty called Pangong Lake. Blue sky and blue water of the lake were amazing.

Earlier, there was one scooter of Karina from the film 3 Idiots but this time I found dozens of them lined up and likewise, there were several sets of three chairs. Of course, I did not find Yak as I wanted my daughter to try mounting a Yak, as I had done on previous occasions. There were definitely more people. Divya was thrilled to see the pristine lake. Unfortunately, we have only 1/3rd of the Lake on Indian side. There were campers also, who watch night sky and felt as if the stars were within their reach.

Divya at the majestic Pangong Lake

My readers must be wondering why I have not mentioned even a word about Chang La. In fact, we simply passed by it. I had been there earlier. Sudesh felt the need for Oxygen and had taken a few puffs from the Cylinder carried by us. She was a little wary. My daughter had in mind conquering Khardung La, as higher aim was in focus, so who cares for the others. Also, after the Lake-stop, we were still required to carry on for another 5 hours to reach Nubra Valley, our 2- night halt. It is a cold desert, and one finds domesticated Double Hump Camels, originally from the Gobi Desert and used to be part of Silk Route Travellers. So, we headed for Nubra Valley. Road mostly was fine but under repair work was going at many places and again curvaceous roads requiring driving skills and full attention. Siachen Warriors had put their name at various places. It was in Nubra Valley we also found Sign Boards': "K 2 to Kanyakumari Bharat is One". K-2 is in POK and is the second highest mountain in the world (Karakorum 2), after Mount Everest. I distinctly recall from my Karachi days (67-70) that K 2 used

I have Resolved NOT to Stop

to be a popular brand of Cigarette and thus Pakistanis used to portray that K 2 is part of Pakistan (as distinct from illegally occupied POK). That is what I had mentioned as a change while describing Hon'ble MP from Ladakh being at the Leh airport where people were carrying Vessels of water from Kanyakumari.

Divya and Sudesh ji at Changla Peak at 17688 FT

Sign of Siachen Warriors on Way to Turtuk

Our nights were going to be in officers' mess and a very cozy place near flowing water body and close to the place where Double Hump Camels camp for rides. It had been a long day and we were also supposed again to be on a long march the following day, so we thought of freshen up after tea and have early dinner and also ask the Mess People to serve us early breakfast and pack our lunch. We were also to arrange mandatory permissions as we had planned to go to the last village close to LOC. After having got confirmation of permission to visit the last village close to LOC, we started early.

Close to Thang Village near LOC

In Nubra Valley there is a River by the same name. It meets the Siachen River. Shyok is its tributary, which is also a tributary to the Indus. Sand Dunes and Leh Berry Shrubs are aplenty there. Leh Berry is thorny shrub and Double Hump Camels like it very much. Leh Berry is a fruit like Raisins but smaller in size and darker in colour. I had taken ripe Leh Berries and found them sweeter and full of nutrients. On the way we met with a group of bikers who needed some tool to fix one of their motorbikes. Luckily, we were able to help them with the tool kit we were carrying. The stop was gainfully used by my daughter to have a short pillion ride on a motorbike to have that experience as well. One can find Camping Grounds and Dessert Bikes for those who wish to spend longer time there or to have that experience of camping in a cold dessert. The average height is 10,000' in the valley. River flows almost at road level (only a couple of feet down) at many places and changing landscapes make for a panoramic view. One can spend days taking snaps.

The drive from our Night Shelter in Nubra Valley to LOC beyond Tur Tuk was beyond description. Awesome scenic beauty, from tarmac road to ditch road, river at places is almost close to road level, deep valley, sharp bends, barren hill tops, blue sky, not a soul for miles, bikers in groups made varied experience in one go. Clay hills, limestone hills and BRO people on work wherever roads required their attention was like a dream coming true of traversing that part of India. I had missed it on my last visit in April 2018. I could allow it to happen again. At Hunder we were told by the BRO team that they had not received a word about our arrival. It appeared that our efforts would go waste but when we spoke to the Army Major in-charge of our trip and that clearance had been sent, he promptly replied that he would check that and after having conversation confirmed that the clearance was there and that he was not informed so that he remained ignorant and now as he knows it, we were most welcome. In fact, he did receive us and offered tea and while handing over the permit slip, he made it clear that we could go up to the last village and on our return, we were to surrender that slip at the post near bridge.

At the Home of Mohd. Khan, Chief of Village Thang near LOC

We came to Village Thang, which is just 2.2 KMs from LOC. Believe me, we did find a tarmac road up to that village and people were all praise for BRO's noble work in keeping their village easily accessible. We went up to the last point and with binoculars could see Village Franu across river in POK. We were welcomed by Village Chief, Mohd. Khan, who literally helped me to take inside his yard, where we were served with water and Rooh-Afza and thereafter, he brought dry apricots and apples. His daughter also brought cut apples and made us feel at home. He also brought a big bunch of grapes and explained that all that was from his orchard. We could also see school children happy in their school uniforms. Flower plants potted in earthen wares were decoratively kept. He explained that he also grows various herbs for medication against various ailments. After a while there was prayer time (Namaz) and he very politely sought our permission to be excused for the prayers and for this he used the word "Pooja" time instead of Namaz or even Prayer. That was the care taken for sentiments of the guests. I wish there were more understanding people like him on earth.

In my write up in foregone para, I mentioned the word "Pooja" used by Mohd Khan of Thang Village Head and I liked it and appreciated that he merely wanted to convey that in his eyes, 'Namaz' or 'Pooja' is one and the same thing. The reverence to God, Almighty, Ishwar, Allah or by whatever name one wishes to call Him or that Supernatural being by whatever name is offered from one's heart will always be answered. Different names were just to understand by different people but in reality, it was one and the same thing. That is what portrays the real Kashmiriyat. It should throng, coming from the head of Village Thang. Before departing from that place, I had asked Divya to give some chocolates and packets of Chewing Gum to the children around. They were almost bewildered to find this gift and I could see 'thanks' in their twinkling eyes.

On the way back, we deposited, dutifully, the permission slip at the indicated check post. We did some snapping on way and returned to our place and stay a little past 3 in the afternoon. It was time for a late lunch for us to go to see Deskit Moastry and herds of double-humped camels. The view of Valley from Deskit Monastery is amazing, and one gets a wide spectrum view of the valley, as to how much nature has been bountiful on it. It was late in the evening by the time we returned. After a while we asked for light dinner; I and Divya were contended to enjoy simmering hot soup. The time for dreaming was approaching, as we were tired and had in mind early start on the following day with aim of being at Khardung La before heading for Leh.

I have Resolved NOT to Stop

Deskit Monastry

It was time to say Goodbye to Nubra Valley. Although I was inclined to go to Hot Springs, but we decided to drop that idea for constraint of time, as after returning to Leh, Jagdish and Sudesh wanted to do a bit of shopping as they were scheduled to leave for Delhi the following day. Yes, on my last visit, I had enjoyed a dip in hot springs and found it a refreshing experience. I was told that the place has now improved facilities. I also distinctly recalled good pastries from a local bakery, we had enjoyed on our earlier visit. At times, one has to adjust as per circumstances. I therefore could not mind missing it but felt that perhaps Divya would have enjoyed the experience.

On the way back of course, we had the high point of our visit to Ladakh in the shape of crossing Khardung La. It is always a thrilling moment. While I was content by craning out my neck out of window of the vehicle, Divya and the rest made it a point to make it memorable by clicking snap after snap. I could see the thrill Divya had on her face. She enjoyed the moments most and also spent the maximum time snapping from various angles of that place. Snowcapped mountains, Buddhist flags adorning that place, the sign boards all caught her attention. She felt exhilarated and for me it was a satisfying moment that I could see happiness on her face.

Revisit of Ladakh and Kayakalp at 76

By lunch time we were back, and after lunch, while I took it easy and preferred to take rest, all others were on a shopping spree. Divya had in mind among other things Reclining Budha, which she was able to fetch along with other items as mementoes of Ladakh. The dinner made us talk over a little about our experiences of the past couple of days. Everyone was happy that the time spent was worthwhile. I also had some new experiences and having covered those places, which I had missed on my earlier visit. While Jagdish and Sudesh left for Delhi, the following day, we had saved that day for local tour, which too has places of interest and in no way, we miss out on them.

On penultimate day in Ladakh was reserved for local landmarks, which are not at all mean or to be ignored. I called Rig Zhin, with whom we had developed good rapport on the previous visit to Ladakh. He is a amiable person and takes care of his taxi like a baby, spic span. That is what I like. He is polite, which most of the Ladakhi people are, I used to call him Rim Zhim (rain). First, we went to see Hemis Monastery. Among other things, it has 12m long Thanka. The setting of almost all the monasteries are such that one has to make an effort to reach there as if Lord Buddha tests whether a devotee has patience or not to reach there. Faith demands patience and practice. We also went to see Shey Monastery and Shey Palace. These present picturesque view from outside. How could we not visit the school of Sonam Wangchuk associated with the movie Three Idiots! Sonam Wangchuk is known for many innovations and for modifying schooling. He is the one credited with Ice Stupas used for storing water during late winters and for use during summers, melting ice provides water for irrigation of fields. The Leh Palace was also covered but before that we also went to see Sindhu Darshan, the place has now become easily accessible by car right up to waterfront. Earlier in September there was a big festival. Leh Palace presents a vivid view of Leh town. The next stop was Kali Mandir, in fact a Gompa and recently come up Vishnu Temple. In a way it was a religious kind of tour, but very satisfying. As Divya had done with Memorial and shopping, we returned back. Rig Zhin shared with me candidly that he would be standing for local elections. He also revealed that the present Hon'ble MP from Ladakh was his classmate and was

I have Resolved NOT to Stop

being prompted to support him in his work. I pray for his success, as good people need to be encouraged.

Three Idiots wall in the School of Sonam Wangchuk

It was also time to pack and be ready for the next morning for onward journey to Himachal Pradesh (Kayakalp in Palampur) via Jammu. On that day Gorav had to leave for Chandigarh but dutifully, he had arranged for our being escorted to the airport. The following day, on 23rd we bid farewell to Leh, remembering well the sacrifices of many to protect our motherland and just to name a few, Capt Anuj Nayyar, Capt. Vijayant Thapar, Capt Vikram Batra; Grenadier Y. Singh, Rifleman Sanjay, Major Sonam Wangchuk, Lt. Balwan Singh, Lt K.C. Nangram, Major Shyam Sundar, Major Vikrant Shastri and Major Vivek Gupta. Most of them were in the prime of their lives, which did not shake them from sacrificing their lives. We remember their past, for that only has protected our future. We were about to head for Palampur, which too had given us Sourabh Kalia, whose body was disgustingly badly mutilated by Pakistanis while he was on patrol and was captured treacherously. Cowardice never pays but bravery never fails. It calls to say Jai Hind and Jay Hind Ki Sena, lines from the immortal song penned by Kavi Pradeep and composed by C. Ramchandra and sung by none other but Bharat Ratna Lata Mangeshkar

A Look at Wayside Shrines in Leh

After bidding farewell to Leh, arrived Jammu by Air India on 23rd September, 2019. Beforehand, my brother-in-law in Jammu had sent SMS to me conveying phone number and car number by which his son would pick us from the airport. Almost 1-hour flight was trouble free and comfortable and as soon as we came out, we were received by Ankur. My brother-in-law, Vijay was insistent that we must come to their place to freshen up and have lunch with them before we start for almost 4-hour drive to Palampur. Thinking that it would also provide us opportunity to meet other members of the family, we had accepted the invitation. Having learned that Divya would like to have Lotus Stem (Kamal Kakri/Bhis/Bhain) or Nadru of Kashmir on her platter, it was specially made, among other things. Apart from Kadam (Ganth Gobhi) and Rajmah among vegetarian dishes, Nadru is also very popular. It is really tender over there. Divya was delighted to see special treatment being given to her. I also exchanged views about ground realities in that part and was assured that things were slowly but steadily becoming normal. It would take some time, but it would be for the overall good of the country.

After having a lavish lunch, the pre-arranged taxi was called to drop us off in Palampur. We were also gifted special Rajmah (Red Kidney Beans) from Bhadrwah. They are really delicious and less sticky than other varieties. Of course, we also gave a few gifts to the family.

I have Resolved NOT to Stop

We could reach Kayakalap only around 7 P.M. As I had already made the booking, we were given key of the room. After a little rest, it was time for dinner and retiring for the night, as the next day we were supposed to be woken up at 5 A.M. for hot water for drinking, freshen up and be ready for Yoga, Pranayam and Laughter Class from 6 A.M. Divya was well prepared for that and in fact was looking forward to a 3-day regimen of treatment and simple meals. Of course, my younger daughter, Surabhi with her own younger daughter, Tripti had also arrived a day earlier to have the experience. Tripti was also interested in doing paragliding for which Palampur has good facility. This arrangement allowed both sisters to have more time together, out of the short span of holidays of Divya. I of course slept like a log after day-long travel.

The day started as scheduled with Yoga. Divya liked the set up there and also the ambience of that place. Dhauladhar mountain range in the backdrop, moderate temperature, a well landscaped campus, helpful people, and simple meals all were to her likings. I having been a repeater knew the place well and had chosen it specifically to showcase it to Divya. She liked various treatments in the form of massages - Potli Massage with herbs, oils, Panchkarma, Shirodhar. She would avoid Jacuzzi as this facility was available in her own at home also. Aromatic Steam bath she liked.

She had developed a taste for various types of Chutneys and soups which were prepared there, as also for Ragi Roti. Herbal Tea she liked. Above other things as mouth freshener and to help digest food, the kitchen had Shakkar (Brown Raw Sugar) and Ajwain (Ajinomoto seeds). Sweet and Bitter combination really helps in digesting food that otherwise is light, without much of spices, and gets easily digested. Of late, she has not been eating non-vegetarian food except fish and that too her present trip she had not tried.

In the afternoons she would again keep herself busy with some kind of treatment, and around 4 p.m. there was time for fruits and some kind of boiled water, like that of Barley, Mint, Ginger and Tulsi (Basil), Coriander (Dhania). Evenings, she would not miss attending a deep meditation session and found the experience to be of of much help.

In the meantime, Surabhi and Tripti wanted to make the best use of their time by going paragliding and returned much thrilled about the experience. Tripti had not much interest in massages, and she wanted to have experiences in Palampur/Dharamshala as such. Time was short otherwise, MacLeod Ganj and an audience with the Dalai Lama was on her list.

On September 25, Surabhi, Tripti and Divya took permission to go on a city tour. After morning treatment, all of them headed for a trip around the city and see tea gardens and other things for a couple of hours as that was the only time Surabhi and Tripti had to spare before they were to head for airport to catch a flight back to Delhi. They left around 11 a.m. and after dropping back Divya, they headed for Dharamshala/Kangra airport, an hour's drive from Kayakalp. I was content with taking it easy.

The rest of the day passed in normal routine, and the following day it was time for us to pack and return home. I know 3 days is too short a period to have the full benefit of Kayakalp but that was the maximum time Divya could spare. The following day we too headed for the airport around 1 p.m.; Kangra and Dharamshala have the same airport. It is neat and clean and greenery around it with good landscaping make it pleasing to eyes and world class for a domestic airport. The cricket stadium there I am told is also excellent and enjoyed by both the spectators and players alike. Surabhi, of course had had that experience earlier.

I wish there was more time available with Divya for Kayakalp as she was really enjoying it but there is always a next time. May be on next visit she will be able to concentrate on it.

After her return there were hardly two days left for Divya to do her shopping and packing. Many items in mind were left, and she headed back home to the US on the night of the 28.

I have been coaxing my son also to come with family to enjoy a stay together and spend some refreshing moments at Kaya kalp. My daughter-in-law is also keen to have Kerala type massage. I have been promised a visit as early as early next year. In the meantime, festival season is near in India and thereafter it would be in US, therefore I wished all a happy Dussehra and other festivals and Season's Greetings.

Ever relevant. I also distinctly recall that during my visits to Ladakh, among other things, somehow, I noticed that the wind which blows makes the sound of 'Om Mani ....'. Some may say it was just imaginary or merely I am developing some kind of myth, but believe me, it is so serene over there that one finds a solace and calming effect in the air. Whatever it may be, it should bring peace and human development so that human beings are able to discover and enjoy themselves face-to-face with such natural wonders.

At Statue of Unity

I have Resolved NOT to Stop

Self during Visit to Rani ki Vav

7th chapter

Gujarat Visit at 78

Pack of History, Culture, Natural Grandeur and Modern India

For a long time, I was looking forward to find an opportunity to visit Gujarat, as during my stints in Karachi (Pakistan), Harare (Zimbabwe) and Dar es Salam (Tanzania) I have had chance to interact with people from Kutch/Gujarat though I was not able to visit Gujarat. Of course, I have crossed Gujarat on several occasions and even seen a number of stations but I never got an opportunity to see closely any part of Gujarat. No doubt, I have had, Gathia and Jalebi, Sheer Khand, Gujarati Kadi, Thepla, Bhajia, Khichdi, Chat and God knows how many other dishes, but to have them at the place of their origin carries altogether a different experience and I was always open for that. I do not mind myself becoming a Guinea Pig but savor I must different dishes. Statue of Unity, Rani ki Bav, Somnath and Dwarka were naturally other attractions in my mind and I was also determined not to miss Rann Utsav. Once an opportunity was presented to me, I could not hold back myself back and promptly grabbed the opportunity.

So, here I decided to once again take the opportunity offered by Senior World though first, I was a little apprehensive about standard of their services not remaining the same as a couple of years back. Anyhow my apprehensions were broadly quelled when, on the appointed day and time, their Tour Manager met 19 of us at the Indira Gandhi airport. The group consisted of people coming from Lucknow, Bareilly, Noida, Chandigarh, NCR Delhi etc and enjoying retired lives hailing from different professions. The flight was as per schedule and after having checked in for the Indigo flight, the wheel chair with attendant was provided to take me swiftly to the departure gate. Incidentally, one of the couples, Jaiswal's, had earlier done a trip to Sikkim with me, and it definitely added to my joy.

The flight was trouble free, and we landed at Vadodara Airport on time. After the collection of baggage, we were made to sit in an AC bus and arrived at the Royal Orchid Hotel. Rooms were pre-allotted and swiftly we arrived in our rooms with our respective partners. The baggage too was brought promptly thereafter. After refreshing tea with some munching's in the hotel room itself we reassembled in the lobby after taking rest for an hour. The first destination was the Royal Palace of Gaikwads in Vadodara (or Baroda). A part of it still serves as Living Area of the ex-rulers. The architecture of the palace built in the latter part of 19th century boasts of one of the largest palaces (including garden area) and has architectural features of Hindus, Muslims, Jains and British (Gothic) styles. Therefore, there are Domes, Pillars, Carvings, Jharokas etc. One can enjoy recorded running commentary in English/Hindi/Gujarati etc on hand-held machines taken by the organizers of the tour from the Palace Reception, where one can reach after crossing a small garden in the courtyard and after showing one's ticket provided by the Senior World. There was a nice painting on the outer wall of the palace, where a group snap was taken as a token of our real journey having been started. Taking photographs inside the palace was not allowed and if caught a person has to pay a hefty fine of Rs. 5000/-, However, one can take photographs from outside the palace. There was a good collection of arms, palanquins, Pictures/Photographs of ex-Maharajas, paintings by Raja Ravi Varma, Italian/Chinese Vases, Ivory, Figures, Massive Chandeliers etc. There was a massive Durbar Hall for ceremonies. There was a cafeteria too in the palace to relax and enjoy hot coffee and snacks.

There were ponds, sprawling backyard.with statues, figures and one was allowed to take snaps from there. Here parties used to be organized by the Royal Family. The garden has a variety of trees, like Amaltass, Tamarind, Drum Sticks, Palms. Nearly two hours spent there passed very fast and each moment took us to the era when the royal family members were busy in passing their disciplined lives, from horse-riding to retiring during nights.

At statue of Unity

Incidentally, Baroda State was one of the five states whose rulers were entitled to 21-gun salute under British Rule and was the third richest state. It expanded up to the coast near Dwarka and included Surat, the hub of the diamond industry. Baroda rulers had good relations with the British and understood the importance of education, which was made compulsory. Understandably, Vadodara gets its name from Vata (Banyan Tree).

After visiting Lakshmi Vilas Palace the group went to see a garden nearby. After returning it was time for an early dinner in the hotel itself, which catered well laid out Buffet (veg and non-veg). Incidentally, Gujarat is a Dry State but visitors can buy liquor with easily available permits. However, the price tag on all brands was rather high. One was not allowed to carry liquor from outside the state even as checked-in baggage.

After having had a good night's rest, the following day was to see the world's tallest statue; Statue of Unity (of Sardar Vallabh Bhai Patel). The main designer, Suthar was then in his mid-90s. He was assisted by

I have Resolved NOT to Stop

his son. It faces Narmada Dam and East so that Sunlight glows and supposedly, Sardar Patel in statue form could see the dam, which was his brain child. Though he did not survive to see fulfilment of his dream project, the designer visualized it as having accomplished satisfactorily the project to serve as a tribute to Sardar Patel. The work on Narmadariver and Safari Park nearby was going on. Eventually, boat rides will be available and understandable have started ferrying people. At pre- appointed time only the visitor(s) were allowed to visit the Statue Site. No beverages or food was allowed inside. Paid wheel chairs were available. Once inside the main entrance, free wheel chairs, if someone can arrange their pushing for you were also available. For going from the main entrance to the statue, there were also automatic walkways. There is a good distance from parking lot of the bus to the entrance in the statue itself. Express lifts take one to the heart of the statue and one can see Narmada Dam and River. Mammoth size of the statue can be visualized from the fact that each button made on the vest of the statue was the size of a main-hole lid. One can go up to the foot of the statue by climbing stairs of two-storey house. There was also a museum in the basement.

I may add here that in the morning at Vadodara Hotel we were also joined by our local Guide, Rajvendra Rathore aka Raj. He throughout the tour described, various aspects of places of our visit, including customs, attire, profession. He became an important and integral part of the troupe and at the sametime we introduced ourselves. It was quite a diversified group and solidified my belief that if there was a will, one can enjoy company of persons with different tastes, likings and moods. There is no compulsion to bear someone but one can get inspired by someone's goodness as to my mind no one is totally devoid of some good points. We can always concentrate on one's goodness. By the way, apart from myself the troupe consisted of me, my room partner, Subhash Chandra Vidyarthi from Lucknow. Before commencement of the tour, he had called me from Lucknow to introduce himself. A fine gesture to acquaint He too was a widower like I and retired Engineer from PWD in U.P. He was the livewire of the group. He was a good photographer and used to take photographs of even strangers.

Gujarat Visit at 78

There was also a couple from Lucknow, Ajay Singh Tomar and Jyotima Tomar. He was retired Chief Engineer from the UP Electricity Board. Fine and Polished persons. Ajay participated in discussions and came out with spontaneous Couplets and Jokes. Likewise, Jyotima could sing and dance well. Sunil Chandra Singh Bisht and Geeta Bisht from Noida were the next. While Sunil had taken retirement from Oriental Insurance, Geeta was still working. Sunil also paints and was quite passionate about it. Quite a gentleman and would take part in conversations Jaiswals was another couple from Noida and were with me during Sikkim trip. From Bareilly we had Subhash Chandra Kumar, who had retired from Sugarcane Department. His partner Usha Sakhuja was well equipped with self-made savories and of course additionally she was accomplished dancer. There was also Dr. Sachi Arya who had presented her thesis on the works of Mahashewta Devi. She took notes as she was an accomplished blogger. She shared her room with Sudha Puri. There was Rekha Dogra from Chandigarh and remained mostly with her room partner, Rachna Mehra. Ms. Ellora Bagchi, who had retired as Asstt. Commissioner, Commercial Taxes was settled in Ajmer. She was a thorough gentle lady and brimmed with positivity. She was quite knowledgeable and conducted herself with dignity and poise. Who can forget intellectual Dinesh Prasad Saxena and his wife Swarn Lata Saxena? How can a group be complete without a turbaned Sikh! So, we had quite jovial Harendra Pal Singh accompanied by Asha Bansal. He was quite an entertainer and participated actively in conversations and would narrate jokes and anecdotes. Always ready to extend a helping hand. He literally pushed my wheel chair on several occasions for long durations. He had his business in Kuwait and was now living near Ludhiana in an old-age home, which according to him was well provided. I was the spoiled child. My difficulty to climb bus or walking, both physical and psychological were taken with due sympathy (not pity) and everyone came out with helping hand. I was literally pampered. Ofcourse I missed quite a few places to visit where climb was tedious, too long or steep, for which I have no regrets. I am always thankful to all those who helped me to overcome my genuine difficulties. I have purposely included a brief description of my group mates, so that I could be able

I have Resolved NOT to Stop

to deal with them in a fair manner if and when we happen to be meeting sometime in future. We could pass our free or long travel time in merriment and without any difficulty and in fact, doubled our enjoyment because of this wonderful company. Future may bring us together, if not all but a few only. Good time spent can be cherished by reminiscing sweet memories.

Let me also share that on the 2nd day of our tour, it took us nearly 2 and a half hours from our hotel to reach the Statue of Unity. If one stays close to the Statue of Unity for which there are ample options, one can see statue in the evening as also when sun rises. This presents more panoramic view. The ticket cost of Rs. 1030/- per person (includes visit to the upcoming Valley of Flowers) was well spent. One can have lunch in one of the way side restaurants. For morning/evening's panoramic view from outside one would be well dvised to check-in, in a nearby hotel in advance and next day (same day 2 of the tour) can go in the first batch to see the statue from inside. I am purposely not giving various measurements of this 182 meter tall statue, which among other thigs used 70,000 tonnes of cement, 18500 tonnes of reinforced steel and 6000 tonnes of structural steel. Post Lunch at the Food Court of Statue, there was a quick round of the Valley of Flowers for which one had to first visit the Narmada Dam site so as to take a connecting bus to the Valley of Flowers. Since, for this trip your own vehicle was not allowed.

During both the drives from Hotel to the Statue and from Statue to Ahmedabad one passed by many water bodies but hardly polluted. Fields and cattle herds could be seen. One could see fields of cotton and castor and a number of drumstick trees. Well maintained roads made the journey a pleasure. Before taking the national highway, we stopped to have tea and refresh ourselves. Though there was sign of Samosa in the Menu, it was not available and instead we were suggested to take Alu-Parantha, which indeed quite a few local folks were enjoying. We were content to have biscuits and chips. Music and gossiping made the journey enjoyable.

On return, by now the familiar drill of retiring to rooms had followed and the arrival of our bags was completed. After a little rest and refreshing ourselves, it was time to have once again lavish buffet dinner. The rooms were always cozy and well-equipped/provided. Good night shelter is always a big boon and takes away the tiredness of the day.

One thing I noticed in Gujarat was that there were definitely few beggars than in many other cities. It does not mean that there were no beggars at all. Of course, I had seen an old tribal lady trying to stop vehicular traffic to seek alms but surely such scenes were rare. By and large, people were engaged in making and selling craft wares. I saw people making Kites, Necklaces, Purses, Colourful Thread (Manjha) for flying kites besides eateries. At one place I purchased a couple of Duppattas and on coming back, I found them to have been made out of old Sarees by adding some smartly made flowers of thread. I won't say I got cheated. Pollution was less and so was litter. I do not say that there was no litter at places but, yes, far too less. For Manjha, apart from powdered glass, rice and jaggery are used. Being close to Makar Sankranti time - Kite Festival time, these things were visible for obvious reasons. While in northern India, there are plenty of castor plants but hardly any organized plantation, in Gujarat I found it as organized farming. Singdana (Groundnuts/Peanuts), Til, Mustard, Jeera (Cumin), Anis (Saunf) apart from cotton crops were there. Fields of wheat and paddy were also there. Milk production and consumption are high. I did find Buttered Milk in various flavors, Curd, Mostly Amul Butter unlike freshly churned white butter as at Dhabas in the north, e.g. (Sukhdev Dhaba on GT Road), near Sonipat in Haryana. Somehow, I did not come across Sheerkhand, the traditional and customary postre(sweetdish) of Gujarat, which is made by squeezing curd with added sugar/or crystalised sugar - Mishri and saffron. Perhaps saffron having become out of reach of a common man, mainly Traditional Mukhwas (like Dhana, Tamarind Seeds, Anis, Crystal Sugar (Mishri) were of course served. One could also find sweetness in dishes like Sambhar/Dal for that is the way Gujaratis like their dishes. Dhokla, Bhajias, Thepla etc were plenty. One could also find a lot of shops selling varieties of Namkeens and Sweets. I know I have not started describing explorations of the day, which will now follow for I understand inquisitiveness has been risen

I have Resolved NOT to Stop

Re-embarking on the real journey of 3rd day (9th January), after morning chores and having had bellyful breakfast, we sat in the bus. A head count was taken, and we proceeded towards Seth Hateesingh's Jain Temple dedicated to the 15th Tirthankar. It was really an architectural marvel.

Our next spot was, ofcourse, not missable, Sabarmati Ashram on the banks of Sabarmati River. Apart from original cottages dedicated to Mahatama Gandhi, Vinoba Bhave and Meera Ben, there were also some structures to accommodate Photo Gallery, etc which were added by famous Indian Architect, Charles Correa, who had designed it. I also recall that in New York too, the building accommodating Permanent Mission of India to the UN and residential complex was crafted by him. Peaceful atmosphere was there despite quite a good number of visitors. In fact, there were a number of budding photographers from Nirma's Academy (mostly girls), who had been thronging the place and were taking snaps of all and sundry. I too was snapped by a girl, who took my permission politely. If it would appear somewhere in some publication, I do not know for despite promise, I was never forwarded the same. Some of us took time to try their hands at spinning wheel. As I am not cleft so I did not make a try. Yes, there was a batch from an NGO working on sanitation and cleanliness. The boys and girls after visit sat down to make some sketches/posters to promote both. Real Leaders do leave a legacy for spreading good in the society.

At Sabarmati Ashram

Gujarat Visit at 78

Our next halt was the Calico Outlet. Having become a sack in width, I could not find typical Kathiawari Jacket of my size. The things were excellent but rather heavily overpriced. Incidentally, the Calico people have collection spanning over 500 years and at a time they can accommodate a maximum of 30 visitors. It was another matter that I have no craving to spend heavily on vintage, as I cannot claim myself as an art connoisuer. We also tried Khadigram Asharam's shop. However, I would not say that the same things were not available in other similar stores. On top of that the owner was of the adamant type unlike Gujarati businessmen in common. There was difficulty in making selection. Somehow some of us were able to manage to shop for a few things and I too picked up a couple of typical lady's handbags for gifting to children.

Invention is the mother of necessity, and the shortage of water had been tackled in by harvesting rain water. The structures built were generally in the shape of step-well and were known as Vav or Bav (Bawadi or Bawri). There was one in Ahemedabad itself just 3 Kms from the Railway Station and it was supposedly 500 years old and was known as Dada Harir Ni Vav. However, we chose to visit 5-storey Adalaj Stepwell (Vav), which was around 19 Kms from the Railway Station. Sandstone walls and pillars have carvings of leaves, flowers, fish and other ornamental patterns.

After the visit, people got tempted to buy Guavas, which were pink from inside and were really sweet with good aroma. Black Grapes and Beries were also bought by some people. Gujarat produces a lot of Plums (Ber) of different varieties both from shrubs and thorny plants from the size of green grapes to as large as good size lemons/eggs. However, they were not sweet or perhaps ready for eating and in fact sticking to throat.

Our next stop was in the new capital of Gujarat (Gandhinagar) around 28 Kms from Ahmedabad Station, the famous Akshardham Temple of Swaminarayan Sect. In its construction 6000 tons of pink sandstones had been used. No eatables or cameras were allowed inside the sprawling temple complex. Guards allow straight access to persons who have any physical challenge. Wheelchair was also

I have Resolved NOT to Stop

available. The garden area has been well kept with various figures made of plants, like elephants, Kalash. Everything seems orderly and well kept. Inside the temple authorities run cafeteria and a souvenir shop. The highlight was water/fire and musical laser show. It became really cold as water came close to sitting benches and it was windy late evening. Infact, whenever there were scenes with fire, some relief from cold was being felt even though we were well equipped. There were two real characters on the huge stage. The story taken was of Nachiketa, who skillfully persuades Lord Yama to reveal reality of Death. It was really every dime spent and can said to be a 'Paisa Vasool' show.

Before alighting the bus for the return trip, I was helped by good ladies, like Sudha Puri, Rachna Mehra to purchase typical Ghaghra-Choli for my grand-daughter from shops in front of Akshardham and I consider it the best buy of the trip, both for price and design. Conveying mere big thanks did not appear sufficient, so, I told them to take a rain check for a treat.

By the time we returned to the Hotel Fairfield by Marriot, it was 9.30 PM and time for a quick fresh-up and dinner. I could not hold myself for long and went to deep sleep instantly.

I must also add that it was my dear Rafiki, Harendra Pal Singh, who pushed my wheelchair during the Akshar Dham Tour. It was really great of him. The tradition of servitude without any qualms or show, he practiced. Of course, later on it was the Tour Manager, Gurpreet Singh, who took this onus on him. Talking about tradition, Guajarati too have carried and maintained their traditions, wherever they have gone or even settled, like in East Africa, where their dress, food habits, rituals, Garba/Dandiya, customs do not find much change. It is not that Gujaratis have not changed with times. Of course, they have. I think, they take to and adopt scientific/technical or knowledge-based technical advancements fast and first while continuing with their eating habits, rituals, customs, etc. So much so, I recall that in Africa, even the Africans knew many Gujarati words for food items, like Bhajia for Pakoras and many vegetables, which Gujaratis introduced there. Perhaps, coastline and traders coming to Gujarat from Africa and West

Asia inculcated in them adaptability, but up to a limit. Much before Vasco De Gama's discovery of India, Arab traders were visiting ports there. Since visitors used to be fewer in numbers, they picked up more from Gujaratis, while Gujaratis also adopted certain things from them. Even some Africans came as slaves with Arab invaders and quite a few are still there, e.g. Sidhis from East Africa. They had even established their fiefdom, Janjira. Sidhi dance, Ngoma (Pronounced Goma) has some similarities with Garba. Both have some spiritual touch beside the drum beats. Gandhi ji supposedly spent a couple of nights in Tanzania en-route to England. Bank of Baroda used to be prominent bank in East African countries. During my tenure in Tanzania, when the MD of Bank of Baroda, Dr. Khandelwal wanted to re-open their branch in Dar-es-Salam, which had been nationalized, we did facilitate the necessary governmental approvals and its re-opening. Diamond Artisans of Surat, textile export from India confirm that they benefited from each other. Cooperation and mutual understanding are essential ingredients for progress and advancement of communities that interact.

At Rani ki Bav

I had somewhat sidetracked our trip to Gujarat. Now coming back to the main journey, we left by bus a little past 9 a.m. after a fully satisfactory breakfast for Patan to see Rani ki Vav (Step Well). We were to cover around 125 Kms which were going to take us nearly three and a half hours. Singing, swinging and happy-go-lucky party went on, cracking jokes and anecdotes, while passing through fields of cotton, castor, mustard, which had started to grow after germination of Cumin. Ofcourse there were a lot of Babool trees, which Camels like for leaves. We also saw herds of camels and cows. Muslim Maldars own most cattle and they are fond of heavy gold jewelry. I saw ladies selling gum from Babool apart from Bers (China Date or Ziziphus Mauritiana).

Rani ki Vav was built by widowed Udaymati of the Chalukaya Dynasty from 1022 to 1063 AD on River Saraswati. Siltage had covered it and it came to re-light around 6 decades ago. Archeological Survey of India started restoring it. In 1990s it was declared as World Heritage Site and it has been adopted for upkeep by Akshar Travels Pvt. Ltd. of Gujarat along with a couple of other such sites, e.g. Sun Temple of Madera. The sprawling lawns and pathways have appeared. Electronically operated machine entry will also start shortly. Entrance and parking areas are being done up. It now finds place of pride on new 100 Rupee Currency Notes of India. The Vav is 7-story from underground to ground level. The 10 incarnations of Lord Vishnu (including Lord Budha) have been depicted by carving on sandstone. Some other saints etc have also been shown.

Patan was also famous for Pure Silk and Zari Patola Sarees. It is believed that there are three families who were real keepers of tradition of double Ikat Saris. A real Patan Patola Saree costs in 6 figures. It is intricate and time consuming art work, where there is no place for even a single mistake. Of course, we went elsewhere to learn basics of elementary Patola.

It was time for Kathiawari Lunch. We ate lunch. In Gujarat no meal is perhaps complete without Chutney/Pickle/Papad. One can find Punjabi dishes/cuisines being offered but I would not advise to order and get disappointed. Clear Butter (Ghee) and Gur (Jaggery) are also common. Some use sauver Bers while frying Dals etc. to give it a tangy taste. Having been satisfied with Lunch the party marched towards Madera to see the famous Sun Temple. The landscape was more or less unchanged. Though, it is no match to Konark, it cannot be left out either for its carvings, which also include some erotic figures. There is a big size pond attached to it. It presents a panoramic view and establishes that Indian artisans have no match when it comes to weaving, jewelry, carving, music etc. The focused work, perhaps, finds its roots in mythology or spiritual philosophy Indians have been practising over centuries.

At Little Rann of Kutch

After having visited nearly a millennium old Sun Temple at Madera built by Chalukaya King Bhimdeo, it was time again to march onwards on Kutch Highway to reach Bajana. Bajana was a Muslim principality. The journey was to take two hours. Evening had started approaching and a chill had started setting in. Chit-chat, munching provided some relief but real relief was at a way side small restaurant, whose owner was busy making fresh ginger tea. Need proved that it was the best tea we have had during entire trip. It was piping hot, strong/thick, aromatic and rightly sweet. To my mind the milk used for making tea makes the difference. Fresh milk is generally a guarantee of good tea. Those who wanted to ease the pain could also do so. Industrial areas would appear intermittently otherwise, we came across the same landscape, as earlier. At places road work would slow down traffic. Before Bajana, there was a Railway Crossing. Luckily, it did not delay us. Little Rann of Kutch was on one side. We were lodged in Royal Safari Camp. It was really a cozy place. It was supposedly spread over 50 acres but at present, 16 acres were being used to accommodate guests in individual

I have Resolved NOT to Stop

self-contained and fully provided cottages. Pathways and land-scaping were superb. While one could have tea/coffee in one's room itself, there were two dining halls for Food, which was freshly prepared from farm-fresh ingredients. The place boasts of old vessels, antique artefacts, e.g. old radio, which add to its value. Traditional furniture, low light, a lit path and the food of Kutch made an otherwise tiring day refreshingly fresh. After dinner it was time to dream of next day's itinerary, which included, among other things, Wild Ass Sanctuary

Morning chores were quickly done and freshly prepared breakfast was taken as there was excitement to visit Little Rann of Kutch to see wildlife and especially the famous Wild Asses. In Gujarat, horses of Kathiawar are also famous, as of Sind (which are smaller in size). Rann of Kutch is otherwise also known as bird sanctuary during winter for Siberian Cranes. The wild asses on last count were close to 5000. They are peculiar for two main features, they are larger and stronger than asses elsewhere and their backs and upper face is brownish. They have become aclaimatized to sustain 1°cof winter cold and 40 Degree C in summer. Other animals were Fox, Jackals, Neel Gaye (a kind of antelope) and birds like Swan, Geese, Siberian Cranes, Pigeons, Eagles, etc. Ofcourse there are different breed of fishes and crocodiles in large salty water body. The distance from the hotel to the Sanctuary was not much, and the Tour Manager and the Guide had made sure that before we reach, they were ready with the necessary permission and tickets.

Bunga in Rann of Kutch (Hut with modern facilities)

Thrilling Moments in Little Rann of Kutch or Cruising in open jeep in Chilly Morning of Little Rann of Kutch

After getting the signal for necessary entry permission from the authorities, the party waiting at the hotel was ready, properly attired in woolens and alighted open jeeps to have a first hand view of the much-talked, Little Rann of Kutch. It was chilly morning and within minutes we were in a vast sandy field spread over miles and as we proceeded further on one side we could see a large water body with flocks of birds, including migratory. It was really spectacular. We were in three jeeps and believe me only after minutes if one jeep was at a little distance, it was hardly visible. There were Babool trees. and intermittently there were groups of shrubs. There were only a few blades of leafy vegetation on the grounds, which are chewed by Wild Asses. We were able to see a Neel Gaye running around and of course three flocks of Wild Asses. They were looking really majestically shinning and strong and running really fast. Some birds were floating and some birds were flying. We were able to see even Siberian Cranes and ordinary cranes, Geese, Swans, Pelicans, as also some other birds, including Eagles. It was thrilling. We drove a few miles around and came close to a mound, which was like watching table or tower. At distance we could also see Watch Towers of the Forest Department as also of Security Forces deployed there to safeguard our borders. It was a really lifetime experience. Having seen a number of forests in various parts of the world, which include the Serengeti, Ngorongoro, etc., I admit there were quite a few numbers of animals or birds than many other places yet it was a different and thrilling experience.

I have Resolved NOT to Stop

On way back we could also see even domesticated animals, like cows, sheep, goats, buffaloes from neighbouring hutments. We could also see some Cumin fields.

On return we found the background yard of the hotel occupied by some locals, who were not only selling Kutchi wares, artifacts, jewelry, purses etc. but I also noticed one of them making necklace from beads. A few of us, could not hold temptation to purchase a few items from them, and I was no exception. After that we were again on march in our familiar bus heading towards Bhuj Hotel. On way we did stop for lunch. Now more industrial units were visible. Apart from other plants in the fields, we also saw Anis (Saunf) plants. Another common item spread on the ground was the waste of tiles. There were a number of units engaged in the manufacturing of glazed tiles.

Group at the entrance gate of Rann Utsav

Regenta Resort was that night's shelter for us. It was located on a hillock and presented quite a spectacular view around. Tastefully decorated and welcomed by refreshing lemon drink gave positive indications of its hospitality. After which, check-in was promptly formalized and for dinner the allocated Restaurant presented a more open view. Content of the proceedings of the day, the sleep during night was also deep and dreaming of more excitement on the following day, which included the Rann Utsav.

Gujarat Visit at 78

As I had mentioned, we saw many industrial units from Bajana to Bhuj. Believe me, I had also picked up from the hotel nearly a 3-feet large Joss Stick (Agarbatti) as it appeared unique and appealed to me as a good memento. It lasts for hours and leaves good aromatic and soothing feeling. For sure we noticed solar panels spread all over places, wind mills. Women appeared roaming without any fear and many of them I saw driving scooties. Use of mobile phones by people appeared quite rampant and even while driving. Every one appeared busy in one's own chores and at least did not see any road rage kind of things. On one occasion I observed that a bike fellow brushed a cycle rider and the latter fellow fell. People just helped both of them without any chaos or Big Tamesha as if it were just an ordinary and acceptable thing to happen when one drives or is on road. We may call it fatalism or appreciating reality or ingrained patience of common people there. No unnecessary fuss or drama. Ware sellers everywhere pester visitors to buy from them. We too faced it at several places and especially as we came out of Sabarmati Ashram in Ahmedabad, we were persuaded by a couple of tribal ladies to buy wares (mostly colourful and decorated hangings with bells and thread-flowers for doors and windows) from them. Haggling of price was there and we did buy from them some items. Now colourful hangings adorn my door, as if almost proclaiming that I have had visited Gujarat.

It is high time to return to the main course of the journey itself. So, as arranged after having a sumptuous breakfast, we deposited our bags with the hotel itself, after packing ourselves with a smaller bag with toiletries, night dress, one dress to change and of course somewhat heavy woollens to be able to fight chilled windy Rann of Kutch, where temperature on an average is 5 Degree C. Around 9 in the morning we embarked by now the familiar bus for visiting our first attraction of the day, namely, Kala Dungari, which is a hillock and the Pakistan border is around just 70 Kms. By now, many of us were with first name terms with co-travellers. The road to this place was curvaceous and rocky. Shrubs, Aak and Babool are the main vegetation and that too scanty. Having fun together we arrived at the parking lot, as the buses are not allowed on the hill. We shifted to locally hired jeeps to reach the top - a distance of around 1 Km. Some came on camel backs and

I have Resolved NOT to Stop

some preferred to walk. There is a temple dedicated to Lord Dattatreya. There were quite a few visitors. There are also a few shops, including eateries. There are a couple of trees. Here tribal people come with their traditional Turbans and ladies Dresses-cum-Duppattas and persuade visitors to have snap attired in their clothes and charge Rs. 20/- for each item given for taking snaps. Many of us did get shot in those attires. I too got snapped with a Kutchi turban and felt like Tribal Leader. The real Kala Dungari spot for viewing border direction was more than another half a Km by alighting some steps and climbing-down some steps on top of the hill, which were necessarily to be done on one's own. It gives a feel of achievement and pride on being so close to Indo-Pak border.

After having more than satisfactory visit to this spot and returning back to the parking lot in jeeps, we were ready to another treat by way of traditional Kutchi Lunch in Village Hodka (Banni). To reach this place we of course covered quite a bit of route taken to reach Kala Dungari and then turned on the road to Rann of Kutch. We entered hut-type Reception but on the back side there was ample room to accommodate and serve almost 50 people in one go. The lunch included among other things freshly made on Angithis wheat rotis and millet Rotla almost drenched in home-made clarified butter (ghee), Kadhi, Bhajis, Khichdi, Dal and of course buttered milk (Chach with cumin and salt). There were also chuttneys, pickle, gur (jaggery). Everything was being served with insistence. The dal was fried with Ber to give it a tangy taste. Of course, there was Vermicelli (Sweetened Sevian in milk) to serve as Dessert. Anis was there as Mukhvas (mouth freshener). It was sheer hospitality and freshly cooked food's aroma which filled our apitite and satisfaction got reflected on the faces of each one of us. The place was owned and served by people from Maldharis, a sub-caste of Muslims in Dhordo, originally from Sindh. After Lunch we proceeded to check-in Mahefeel-e-Rann Resort, owned by Salambhai and Harunbhai. The place has been built in traditional ambience and so decorated but the resort was well equipped with day-to day modern facilities, e.g. A.C., Toilet, Running Water, Geyser, CCTV, etc.

I do hope that my narrative of the Gujarat Trip is not found boring to my readers and that they do not find it self-proclaiming. I am trying to be honest in expressing my feelings and perhaps that may help, if not all, a few to march on a similar journey. To my mind every journey is educative and adds to one's life experiences and at times one may even learn from other's style of living, attire, conduct, behavior, eating habits, etc. and of interest.

Yes, I must tell name of the apparent mud-huts. These are called Bhungas. Bhungas are decorated with wall paintings, from inside and have proper cemented floors and all the modern day luxuries or necessities, including running hot and cold water. The beds are generally decorated and mirror work is there. Walls also carry decorative paintings and ceilings are artistically made with painting, thread-work, painted structure. From outside the roof looks like thatched and acquires look of a hut - round in shape. There are windows and attached modern-day bath. In Mahfeel-e-Rann in which we were lodged had apart from a big parking lot after the entry, big Reception, decorated walls and furniture, mounted pictures. There were around 20 Bhungas, a big courtyard, a stage for artists to perform, a floor for dancing in its front, enough chairs for 50+people to sit and watch performing artists, a big restaurant with a kitchen, hand wash area, toilets, etc. In dessert areas music can be heard from a distance of 1 Km. Without any need for artificial or instrumental amplification. Music is in fact an interwoven part of the culture there. It is also important to know that the musical instruments were invented by them and are still made by musicians. These include Ghado (Earthen vessel - Ghara), Morchang is got made with the help of blacksmith, Ghamelu/Tagaru (big bowl made of iron used for carrying soil/sand), Another important feature is that Ghado and Tagaru are played as if they were male and female part of a pair of Tablas (a pair of drums - percussion instrument). These traditional instruments were used with much gusto. Artists wear turbans and were able to shake and jerk their bodies on rythem. They could sing and swing at a very high pitch. Music is in their blood. After taking tea in Bhunga, we were ready for our much-awaited visit to the Rann of Kutch itself.

I have Resolved NOT to Stop

Colorful camel cart which carried us from Rann Utsav Gate to the Greater Rann of Kutch - Sun setting time

By the time we were having tea, our tour Manager, Gurpreet Singh (GPS) and the guide Raj, arranged for us to have the necessary permits to enter the Rann Utsav area and the real Rann, which is so talked about that no one of us was able to hold any more. After alighting the bus, we came at the parking area near the Gate of the Rann. The distance was not great. However, it was just the gate, we were yet to proceed nearly another 1 Km to arrive at the Rann, the salty, marshy land spread like white sand. We took camel carts to reach the real spot. There was music all around. The camel cart was also well adorned. The cart owner helped people alight the cart and we arrived at the spot. The sun was about to set-in so we could not miss taking snaps, before landing on the sand. The weather had started to become chilly. It was such a fun to walk on the sand, as if we were on a different planet. People were there with their kites for flying. There was also a facility for paragliding. Some people were enjoying that. Some were content listening to music. Some were engrossed in seeing the setting sun. It was like a Fair and there was something for each one of us to enjoy. Even children were busy in bungge jumping. Now was the time to wait for the moon to rise. It was a hazy night, and there were hardly any chances to see moonlit Rann. Still, some of us were insistent and wished to carry on, having come so far and on the spot of main atrraction of the Rann. So, wait was the call. The moon did rise but it was dim moonlight. However, it did not disappoint us. When we were coming back again on camel carts, we saw some people busy in watching the Rann in Car Head-Lights. A number of cars would focus light on Rann. The scene was spectacular but lacked the moonlit whiteness as the cars' lights were somewhat paleish. Nevertheless, it was a great fun. It was time to enjoy music and dinner back at our Bhungas. The local artists were engaged in providing local music and men and women visitors were dancing on their tunes. It was really mystique. The freshly cooked food was tasty and filled our belies with local cuisines served with lavish hospitality. The time for retiring for the night had come and, in the night, we could hear sharp noise of desert winds shattering walls of our Bhungas but surely, we were safe and cozy under wraps of warm blankets and heaters.

What a spiritual experience it provided. One can marvel at the hardships people suffer without such comforts, but take it from me, the local people were happy with the increasing number of tourists and the help in settling down they got from the Gujarat Government. They felt highly obliged and satisfied that they were now leading much better lives and that their Handcrafted articles were now finding many takers. Kutchi wealth of traditional crafts, not only gets reflected in textiles or embroidery, but also in woodcarving, cast silver work, lacquer work, terracotta pottery and even leather work, including on camel hide. Their craftmanship has been acknowledged and honored by National Awards

It was 13th January, 2020, when we woke up that morning after full night's rest. We wished each other Happy Lohri. After morning tea and having finished morning chores, it was time for freshly prepared breakfast. A few snaps were taken in the courtyard of the place and we lodged ourselves in the bus for exploration of Bhuj. On way we had our usual fun, chatting, singing and munching. Bhuj which was vastly devastated on the Republic Day of 2001 was resettled with the resolve of the Government and without doubt fortitude of the people. Being in seismic affected zone, the Government has now introduced strict regulations for buildings and structure to be shock-worthy and guaranteed safe.

The Great Wall of the old fort of Bhuj was still under reconstruction with additional touristic attractions. On top of the hill of Bhuj City there is a temple dedicated to Nag Devi, which was visited earlier by the then ruler on elephant-back with a great fanfare and literally a peacock feather fan in his hand. Before checking in, in the hotel we went to city tour and see old palaces. As these involved steep climbs, I excused myself and instead went to see the old fort wall area. There is a water body in the city. I also saw, apart from other temples, a temple dedicated to Jhulelal, revered by Sindhis. It was later on confirmed by Raj that there is a sizeable Sindhi community in Bhuj. Incidentally, I recalled from my Karachi days that both Sindhi and Kutchi languages are almost similar and in fact the scripts of both are written like Arabic/Urdu from right to left. In Bhuj, however, people were using Gujarati or English. After check-in, in the same hotel and having got back our deposited bags, we were informed by GPS that there will be a Lohri Bonfire in hotel's courtyard. Infact for this, one of us, Sardar P. Singh went in advance to make necessary arrangements, including Peanuts, Revris and Popcorn and bonfire. Yes, we had such a great evening singing, dancing, cracking jokes, Bhangra on Drum Beats....

We went round fire offering Groundnuts, Revris and Popcorn. The traditional song, "Sundar-Mundariye" was chanted. There was music. Photographs were taken. Of course, some local girls and even men joined us as music is in their blood and they could not resist tapping their feet. How could they miss such a wonderful opportunity! I saw a hotel girl making a video of the entire festivity, perhaps, for posterity or showcase as how the guests can enjoy and celebrate.

People must be wondering what about shopping when there were so many handicrafts to choose from. Of course we did this on way. After taking lunch in local restaurants, as per one's choice, I could not resist my temptation of shopping experience. In fact, I wanted to club my journey and shopping experiences, which were really great. We went to two villages, which specialize in making various traditional items. We also saw their huts. Please believe me, appearing mud huts, decorated with wall paintings, they were extremely comfortable in that climate. Modern day facilities and glazed tiles were also used in the toilets. We did buy a lot of things, colourful bags, purses, bed-spreads, jackets, shawls, dupattas and of course necklaces. We also went to see as to how Patola Sarees, Duppatas and Stoles were made. Who can desist craving to make purchases, when wares were unique and from

Gujarat Visit at 78

the source. Patola work was really tiring and hardly pays to the artisans. Many of the artisans were awarded by the President of India. Even in Bhuj, after visit to Aina (Mirror) Palace etc, some of us chose to do marketing of local wares. The things were comparatively cheap in Bhuj, perhaps, owing to competition and high turn over but to my judgment, the work at the villages visited by us was more intricate and of high quality, when one was to judge closely and put it on a sharp scrutiny.

The night dinner was as usual sumptuous and filled our bellies. It was time to take rest reminiscing proceedings of the long day, having discovered various aspects of life in this part of India. Harsh but hospitable Rann of Kutch leaves its indelible imprint on one's mind. It is not at all merely a barren desert, it is colourful, musical and mystique land presenting man's fortitude not only to survive but also thrive with working-imagination, hard work, utilizing time, terrain and even animals for beneficial use, which one can notice in it the story of progress of mankind through various ages and stages.

On 14th morning after having breakfast, we were all set to proceed in our familiar bus to the world heritage city, Amdavad (Ahmedabad). By now, the familiarity with each member of the group, tour manger, guide, driver and even his helper was firm in our minds. We have been enjoying together and with that spirit we started our 7-hour journey from Bhuj. Passing through almost familiar country side. We wished each other Happy Makar Sankranti and after a while started munching Revris and Peanuts. We also played a game of Tambola and luckily, I could also win a prize for the middle line which doubled my investment in the game. It was for the sake of fun and passing time. Singing, music and cracking jokes continued thereafter. We did stop for lunch. We tried fresh sugarcane juice laced with lemon though I also wished to add ginger and mint. As it was one's own choice, I topped it with mango chacch (buttered milk). It was really tasty. GPS shared with me, Samosa. Each one of us was having one's choice. Some of us also purchased some local sweets also.

We were again on our way back and having fun. Some preferred to sleep, for by now the long journey had started taking its physical toll. By 4 p.m. we arrived at the hotel and after having a much-needed

I have Resolved NOT to Stop

welcome drink, we retired to our rooms. Some people of course did go out to meet their acquaintances and some still preferred to do shopping. The famous Jhulta Minar understandably, was no longer open for visitors. Of course, there were some other historical and new sites to venture but perhaps what we had done was enough. It is always better to leave something for future as an excuse to re-visit and remember what was done earlier and go on searching new options. The dinner was by now a familiar affair. Incidentally, I noticed a girl from Manipur working at the Reception Desk and one of the Restaurant Captains from Himachal. On top of that, he happened to be from a locality close to my residence in the NCR.

The following day, after breakfast, we were all set to return back. A couple of us took direct and separate flights to their homes, which included my roommate too. Sardar HP Singh extended his stay in Gujarat. If someone wants any clarification or elaboration, I am always there. Before closing this Chapter, I should not forget to mention that I noticed almost a flood of Pomegranates during the journey at several places. There were heaps of them. Also, during Lohri Festival, we could discover the talent of dancing and singing our group people had. Overall, it was an enjoyable experience with good company, food and much to see and watch and on top of that to bring back goodies for gifting to dear ones and one enjoys the gleam on the faces of those who get gifts and what more one wants for satisfaction in life!

The check-in was swift at the airport, and the flight was on time. We arrived on time at IGI airport. After the collection of baggage, the customary goodbyes were done with heavy hearts and solemn promise to repeat our journey together to some other place and above all remain in touch even after we have departed from the airport. The Tour Manager, Gurpreet Singh Gujar (GPS) touched my feet while saying goodbye, a good gesture! I purposely called him GPS as he was the one to announce the day's and following day's programmes, and also used to give advice as what to expect during and at the destination, exactly as a GPS does. These trips are not merely enjoyable and educational but also keep one fit bodily and mentally. I am sure there will be quite a few takers. However, if someone wants any clarification or elaboration, I can be contacted freely.

I have Resolved NOT to Stop

Traditional Rowing Boat on Naini Lake - Favourite Enjoyment for Tourists - Fun Aplenty

8th chapter

Recalling Lake City Nainital

Charm of Naini Lake remains undiminished.

In connection with UDMRD Society's - NGO, where I take responsibility as its Vice President (Rural Development), forthcoming project for Women's Empowerment in Nainital District, I had a chance to revisit Nainital for two days after a long gap. Chiledhood memories were revived. Many more shops and congestion were visible but basic features of Nainital were luckily intact, especially its main beauty, the Lake. There were many more pucca houses on the way to all the hilltops - Subhash Peak (China Peak), Snow View, Laria Kanta, Tippon Top and others around the Lake. Talli and Malli Tal areas were now more crowded. Luckily the ground near Capital Cinema, where we used to play hockey and where it used to be the scene of cultural programmes and skating on a wooden floor, was more or less intact. It was here that, for the first time, I had heard, famous folk song of Mohan Upreti, "Bedu Pako Bara Masa, Kafal (a sweet-sour fruit) Pako Chaita". It still resonates in my mind, even after more than six decades. New routes have also come up for Nainital and other hill stations around. I recall that when we moved from Mathura to Nainital, the last Railway Station was Kathgodam and from there Nainital by road used to be another 18 miles (around 29 Kms) and it used to be really a tiring journey. The road was really steep, curvaceous and some of the turns were really dangerous. I still remember, one such turn, which used to be called "Cheel Chakkar Mod", which meant Eagle's Whirling Turn and indeed the accidents there were common.

People, however, were still friendly, simple and helpful and big city's cunningness was definitely far too low, perhaps, big cities leave hardly any time with people for self and relax. Nainital used to be the Summer Capital of Uttar Pradesh. It was here again that for the first time, I saw hand-driven, Rickshaw and Pal Boats on the lake. Our house used to be near lake, on its lower side (known as Talli-Tal).

At Naini Lake, Nainital with Col. P.D. Sharma

Surely, it was chilling cold during the night, but we were able to get shelter in Army Officers' Guest House and could enjoy, much needed, our evening drinks and sumptuous and freshly cooked dinner.

I also recalled that during an NCC Camp in 1962, I had visited Nainital, when we were camping in Ghorakhal, near Bhawali. Bhawali used to be just 7 miles from Nainital and was known for a Sanatorium and also for plum, apricot and apple orchards. In that area, there was a huge estate of Nawabs of Rampur and the famous film, 'Mahal', which made Lata's singing of song, "Ayega Aane Wala..." bring her to the limelight became an immortal song. Around that place, there are other important lakes, like Bhimtal. By the way, there are other lakes nearby Nainital, namely, Naukuchia Tal, Sapt Tal, Sukha Tal, etc.

In those days, we used to go on for miles on foot, and it was very enjoyable. It was almost like a picnic every day. Boarding Schools, like Sherwood were quite known. There was a well-disciplined life. I also recall it used to be mentioned by elders that during British Rule, on the Main Road, only the Britishers were allowed, and for others close by near the lake, there used to be a rough road but lower that the Main Road. Apart from Boating, and Horse Riding, Hitch-Hiking was also common pastime. Naini Lake has been shot in many Bollywood Movies. The panoramic beauty of the place remains intact.

On the way back, we picked up Pomelo, Guavas, Sweet Potatoes and above all, I could not resist myself from asking our driver to purchase some sugar cane from a farmer who had a loaded bullock cart. Believe me, I could not stop peeling sugar canes and chewing and sucking the sugar cane juice. Yes, the sugar canes were not as soft and tender as I used to have them in Roorkee in the late 50s (then part of District Saharanpur) - the famous Ponta and No. 312 varieties. One was able to easily peel the skin in one go, from top to bottom. But still, it was a wonderful experience, and succulent sugar cane made my mouth sweet and rich with its fresh taste.

Surely, our rural side has much to offer provided we are ready to grab and more than that promote it. People are generally friendly and helpful. I do hope that we will try to visit these places more often, which are cheaper, provide a wonderful and rich experience, and in our case, it was also reviving childhood memories and one can have unadulterated, fresh fruits, vegetables and above all, also enjoy local cuisines. Moreover, our lungs will get well-pumped to withstand city pollution.

I have Resolved NOT to Stop

At Dev Prayag witnessing confluence of Rivers Bhagirathi and Alaknanda, which form The Ganges

9th chapter

Uttarakhand - Holy and Wholesome at 78

Glimpses and impressions of childhood got practically translated.

The urge to travel and to find a breathing place gets re-kindled from time to time, as I have come to reckon that it is essential to put our ordinary daily routine aside and find something which has remained hidden, if not forbidden, by other constraints and compulsions. I discover an eager child in me longing to go on and on. I am not an explorer, like Columbus, but surely have started getting an urge to find for myself my heaven on earth. I start feeling restive for having not gone out, for a while, as I feel that it really broadens my outlook besides it gives me physical boost to go on enjoying life and learn. Naturally, this made me to go on a tour of Uttarakhand.

If you ask anyone whether he knows about Uttarakhand, invariably the answer will be 'Yes' and even some may add that it was carved out of Uttar Pradesh during Vajpayee ji's Government. I was literally not aware of the immense natural beauty spread all over Uttarakhand despite the fact that I in a way belong to Uttarakhand having spent my childhood and early youth in Roorkee (UK) and in my early childhood I was in Nainital, both were then in UP and now form part of Uttarakhand. The trip was suggested by a dear friend, Meenam Malhotra, who unfortunately, due to an accident with her daughter, could not herself join, at the last minute. A Long spell of virtual inactiveness owing to long spell of Corona epidemic also needed to be broken. So, I decided that I must grab this opportunity and of course by taking all the precautions, like vaccination doses, mask, etc.

We were to be led by a 92-year young expert mountaineer, K.P. Sharma. It in itself was a big inspiration and naturally motivates me even now to go on and Never Think of Stopping. In all, we were 10 people plus the driver, Neeraj. The journey was to start on 30th September 2021 at 06:00 hrs. from Dehradun. Therefore, those from outside, like me were advised to reach Dehradun on 29th September itself. Though by age I was running in 79, yet I was among the youngest in males and there were as many as four ladies, Alpana Sharma, Brij Rani and Indu Kochhar from Delhi and Neerja from Garhwal itself, but having settled there only recently. Apart from KP Sir, there were Murari Lal and Satnam Singh Kundi from Gurgaon, KP's friend Thapliyal from Mumbai and myself from Faridabad and on way in Rishikesh we were joined by Dr. Suman Kumar Sharma, who resides in Hardwar and whose father had settled in Haridwar in 1930s after migration from that part of Punjab, which now forms Himachal Pradesh. Murari Lal and of course our leaders were always full of energy. Satnam Singh Kundi devoted most of his time and attention in photography. The ladies made the trip lively by continuous singing or playing Antakashrihar; and Murari Lal always joined them in singing. Thapliyal was always full of energy and our main food supplier, by way of Bananas, Apples and of course Pahadi Cucumber, which were 5-6 times bigger than what we get here. Brij Rani, too joined in peeling and serving fruits. I could only comment and compliment. It was a self-contained contingent, which was well provided and looked for fun.

KP Sir, a Living Legend and Mountaineer

Gracious KP Sir had invited team members to his house on the 29th, which I had to decline as I naturally preferred to stay with my sister and also meet other relatives in Dehradun itself.

The journey started on time the next day (06:15 hrs) from a pre-decided starting point in a 12-seater van and the driver Neeraj stacked our baggage properly and almost everyone got seat of one's choice. KP Sir preferred the window seat near the gate. All through the entire journey, he remained alert and agile and cautioned us on every important point as to what to expect from the outside. He amazingly remembered each and every corner and even guided the driver. The driver, Neeraj, on the whole was a well-behaved and above that a well-disciplined driver. He would give way dutifully to smaller and speedier traffic and also to the vehicles with emergency services. He used to wait wherever required, e.g. at roadsides when trucks were being filled by BRO men with rubble accumulated from landslides. BRO indeed doing yeoman's work in restoring and even widening roads. Roads were good in general, but it was clear that landslides had left their mark and had caused a tremendous damage. On the whole, it was smooth sailing. Yes, of course, the interior of the van could have been better designed and its seats could have some more additions and comforts. Yes, no doubt, the vehicle otherwise gave us no trouble, not even a flat Tyre. Thanks for His mercy.

Our first roadside stop was Dev Prayag. It is the place of religious importance owing to being the point of confluence of Rivers Bhagirathi and Alaknanda, which form The Ganges. Clicking was done and one could see for quite some distance the two distinct water bodies merging and becoming a force to reckon with. Thereafter, we proceeded to cross the town of Srinagar (distinct from the one in Kashmir). It is seat of State University of Uttarakhand. After passing another town, Gochar, we reached Nagrasu (Rudra Prayag). We also were pointed out an important temple of Dharini Devi. At Nagrasu we had lunch. Some of more enthusiasts went to enjoy Langar Prasad in nearby Gurudwara - Damdama Saheb, which was just around 200 Meters from where we had lunch. The place with Golden Lord Shiva's statue on one side was liked by everyone and so much so when learned that it also has comfortable rest rooms, it was decided to make advance payment and book for one night on way back. Of course, meticulous, KP Sir, himself saw rooms and made a deal when he was himself satisfied about its being a good one night's shelter.

I have Resolved NOT to Stop

With Indu Kochar and Alpana Sharma near Tehri Lake

We passed Karan Prayag and reached around sunset time at our destination of the day, Gwaldam. We checked in Hotel Trishul. I must caution friends that at such places one cannot expect 5-star luxury but yes after day's journey, such places do provide tremendous relief. Meenam through Mobile kept a close watch on the proceeding journey. Satnam also helped in train booking. Neerja and Indu Kochhar proved to be the Lata and Asha duo, as they constantly sang song after song, remembering the lyrics as also the correct tune. M. Lal would often join in star. Ladies also served savories, biscuits, fruits etc almost continuously. We even tried mineral water directly coming from mountain glaciers. We did stop on way to have some relief from heavy bladders and also to click and enjoy scenic beauty and breathe fresh air outside of Van. In the hotel Trishul in Gwaldam, a couple was the caretaker and were indeed from Cleaner, Cook to the Manager. The hotel has only two rooms attached with English toilets. On my plea, Neerja and Brij Rani agreed to exchange room with us (I and Satnam). It was really gracious of them to have understood my predicament and sacrificed their comfort for our convenience. Satnam remains well provided with canned food, like Sardines, Biryani, Mackerel etc. as he does not eat spicy food of the hotels. At best he would take plain type of noodles. He kept his own electric kettle and enjoyed his own brewed tea.

We after wash and our evening poison, we shared meals, including the canned food brought by Satnam. To be honest, I could not have much of cold food, but he enjoyed every morsel of it. I have a snoring problem and I forgot to put on my nose the snoring reducing device. and on the other hand Satnam suffers from insomnia and as a result, both of us were not as comfortable, as we had thought. Thereafter, we used to have single rooms, though I firmly believe in company to chat and enjoy the free time in talking.

I must add that for travellers to Uttarakhand then, it was mandatory to have had at least a fortnight old Certificate for full vaccination against Covid. Of course, for those on Chardham Yatra (Gangotri, Yamnotri, Badrinath and Kedarnath) additionally a 4-day old Negative Covid Test Report was also required. The certificates were checked at the Railway/Bus Stations/Stand. We all were well covered. However, we did not neglect wearing masks. In addition, the driver had also obtained, after gathering information, E-pass for the last point Gwaldam. Our Van was stopped at various checkpoints, and we were allowed to proceed without any fuss, as our destination or itinerary did not form part of Chardham Yatra.

Gwaldam, is situated at 30.02 Degree N 79.57 Degree E. It has an average elevation of 6360', which is between Nainital and Musoouri - both hill stations in Uttarakhand. It was part of the erstwhile Katyuri Kingdom and around 12 miles from its capital in Baijnath. Baijnath again is a common name, as there is one in Himachal Pradesh, and yet another is in Bihar. Of course, all the three are dedicated to Lord Shiva. The temple is worth a leisure visit as it is 1100 years old and there was much to see in such a short place. Its locale was also very nice as river flowed on one side and there was also a dam.

Dam Near Bageshwar

I have Resolved NOT to Stop

The next morning, on October 1, after simple breakfast of Cauliflower Paratha with home-made pickle to down it with tea made us ready for Baijnath and other places. Before proceeding with our baggage after checking out, KP ji did check whether our Van would be able to reach parking spot. It was his habit to check readiness of the place of next visit so that later on there was no hassle. Baijnath was quite a place, being serene and awakening dedication and reverence. People tie-up brass bells seeking blessings of Lord Shiva. On fulfilment the bells are removed. One could enjoy a picnic and make fresh hot food there. The slow pace of water had also a calming effect.

3 ladies of the Group Mocking as 3 Monkeys of Gandhi ji at Anashakti Ashram, Kausani

It was decided to turn to Kausani. It was well-known for scenic beauty, Pt. Sumitra Nandan Pant, the famous Hindi Poet belonged to this place and had written about it. Of course, Mahatma Gandhi had also stayed there. The place was known as Anashakti Ashram. From here peaks of Nanda Devi and other two mountains can be seen on a clear day. Our day presented a hazy picture only. There was also in the neighborhoods a Library dedicated to Sarla Bahan. I must add that in Anashakti Ashram, the joyous Indu joined by other two ladies posed as the three monkeys of Gandhi ji - Bura Mat Kaho, Bura Mat Suno and Bura Mat Dekho. Gents too followed the suit and perhaps, it was one of the finest photographs of the trip. I do not know whether the three

Uttarakhand - Holy and Wholesome at 78

At Anashakti Ashram, Kausani

also got inspired to pose like this or it was just a prank to pretend imbibing Gandhi ji's teachings.

We then proceeded to Bageshwar and finally reached our destination of the day, Hotel Him Shikhar in Chakori which was neat and clean and rated well for its location, facilities and service. After freshening up, evening tea, the evening was dedicated to a welcome trip. It was over drinks (of course both hard and soft and juices). We made sure that there would be no forcing or coaxing for hard drinks and everyone was free to have one's choice. Here too Satnam used to bring his cocktail of rum and coke in a bottle. Saltish and nuts used to add to the enjoyment and of course, cucumber used to add salt to the taste. The time was also utilized to review day's proceedings and plan for the next day, including departure time and accordingly ordering bed tea and hot water, where and when required.

The scenic beauty of the place and on way was really enchanting and enthralling. The greenery was in abundance. There were pine (Cheed) and Deodar trees and at places even Dhak/Teak trees used to appear. The step fields were really adding to natural beauty. In between springs used to spring up welcoming and freshening surprise. Bugyal - pastureland and grazing animals would add to our enthusiasm. Paddy had been cultivated. Lands were being prepared for sowing Wheat crop, if not already planted with peas. Nature charm was spread all over.

I have Resolved NOT to Stop

Before I start my account for 2nd October 2021, I must add that there was a little drizzle in the evening, and I slept trouble-free. Also, on the first day's trip out and in general, we used to get thrilled whenever there would appear snow-capped mountain peak as and when sky was absolutely clear, otherwise clouds used to play pranks. At times, from a distance, white clouds give the illusion of snow. The roads were circuitous and at places patchy. It was sometime uphill climb and sometime a downhill climb. Another thing noticeable was the mile-signs, which used to play games, as at a given point if some distance is shown, at a short distance after that it used to invariably show more distance. It was possible and perhaps the roads were made to take different and new routes/turns. As elsewhere, here too we found people thronging liquor shops. We always found crowd in front of such shops, whether open or about to open. I could also notice that neat and clean village roads were built under Atal Gram Sadak Yogna and also noticed almost sparkling way going to the Clean Village under Atal Yogna. Development is always helpful in lifting up standard of life and even mental health. We too used to ensure that whenever required to take food at the roadside Dhaba/Restaurant. However, we would ensure that it was hygienically clean, and that utensils and plates were clean and we even got them washed with hot water. At such places, generally meal was simple and not too greasy or spicy. Fresh Chapatis were also available.

When part of our team had gone to see 'Kasturi Mrig' preserved by forest guards, Satnam fell and came down, with the help of teammates, limping and holding an iron rod for support. Having learned about it, we had kept hot milk and Turmeric ready to give to him. I also had some medicine, which I insistently made him to take. Thank God, bruise was there but no bleeding or fracture. He too had shown courage and by evening he was as cheerful as ever and started clicking and kicking. Yes, of course, I had almost forgotten about our very dear friend, Thapliyal, the right-hand man of our leader and equally energetic and willing to assist. Occupying front seat, he made sure to jump at the first opportunity to find fruits, relieving place and even good restaurant. Friendly and really sweet person. Hailing from that area, he knew the places and guided us to

Uttarakhand - Holy and Wholesome at 78

Tehri Lake

purchase the specialty of each place, like Bal Mithai - a local sweet, which we of course enjoyed, later on, courtesy Neerja.

Being 2nd October almost all the shops were closed and even milk for Satnam we could find with some difficulty. Some of us wanted to have Beer, but due to the holiday on account of Mahatma Gandhi's birthday, it was not available and there were no Bar/Restaurant serving Beer. It was a Dry Day.

I had mentioned about temple of Dhari Devi. It is on the banks of Alaknanda River between Sri Nagar and Rudra Prayag. While on outward journey, we could see it from upper side of hilly road, on inward journey, we just passed by it. Another important fact about the temple was that its ruling deity, Dhari Devi's upper half of the idol is in the temple, while the lower half was located in Kalimath. There was enthusiasm to see some local produces and products and we were told that near Tripuradevi's temple we can find a big workshop. I am always keen for such a venture, as I feel that thus I would be able to help local workers/artisans. After asking several people, we could reach past Beringag Village, Kumayun Earth-craft. It was a Self-help Group run by ladies, named, AVANI. There were two ladies and very few types of items of Silk and Wool. I bought a woollen stole for my daughter for Rs. 2150/- after discount. It reminded me of Scotland. My appetite for shopping was somewhat calmed but our stomachs were otherwise craving for food. We were looking for food as by then definitely, we started feeling really hungry. We could, courtesy Thapliyal, find a nice restaurant, which was neat and clean and had a good ambience being simply but tastefully decorated. The place had a lot many plants also. One such plant of Rosemary, I mistook it for Lavender, being almost of similar look. The owner was a devotee of

I have Resolved NOT to Stop

Baba Neem Karoli, a renowned religious saint, who was supposedly considered reincarnation of Lord Hanuman. Some of us were keen to have Beer but here too, it was not available, as was the case in the market. Of course, as forewarned by the Cook-Manager of Hari Krishna Kala Hotel of Berinag, he took almost an hour to prepare fresh food especially for us as per our order. It was tasty and like home-cooked food. Everyone enjoyed. He was profusely thanked. The Restaurant's name was also taken after the names of Mother and Father (Ka and La) of its owner. It indeed was a happy experience. We arrived back in Hotel Him Shikhar and waited for the evening get-together in Dr. Suman and Lal's room. In the meantime, we ordered tea to lighten somewhat of tiredness.

Hotel Him Shikhar at Chakori with Dr Suman Sharma

Evening came and almost everyone assembled. It was really a lovely evening with songs after songs, including on my request, some old and rare numbers, which Neerja and Indu sang with ease qualifying for more masterly skill than ordinarily expected. Of course, it indeed also turned out to be a Candle-night affair as there was heavy thunderstorm and rain and the lights had gone out. It turned out to be a memorable evening. Naturally, we disbursed after the enjoyable evening and I for one slept deeply and got up on time next morning for departure at 08:30 hours having cleared our bills the previous evening itself.

On October 3, 2021, it was time to bid bye to Hotel Him Shikhar (Chakori) and proceed to pre-booked Hotel Neelkanth in Nagrasu, where we had taken lunch while on way to Gwaldam. We took group

Uttarakhand - Holy and Wholesome at 78

and individual photographs in front of Van, which also carried the banner suggesting Senior Citizens on Uttarakhand Promotion Tour. We started almost on time, as we were ready having had our breakfast. I must add that Ms. Alpana Sharma was generous in providing tea/coffee and even sandwiches, like Indu used to feed us with Kachoris. Our hands and mouths were always full and so were our stomachs. Alpana also used to add comments and buck-up the singing group. She also used to hum and even suggest songs.

The village in Gwaldam under Ideal Village Scheme was named as Gwaldam Talla, which literally means Lower Gwaldam. For its height from sea level, It could have even be called Upper Gwaldam, as if it were Gwaldam Malla. In Berinag we had learned that Trout fish was available on way to Nagrasu from Chakori. However, our search and enquiry at several places turned to be in negative as by that time fresh fish had already got sold. One fellow had but only a couple of hundred grams, which was totally insufficient and would have presented dilemma as whom to serve (after getting prepared) and whom to deny. Yes, of course, the other wish of some members to have beer for evening at the hotel was fulfilled, as on way, we were able to buy Beer. Once again, the brave Thapliyal was the hero who walked a few yards up to the shop and come back with the booty. Lal of course joined him. There were always such occasions when one gets what one wants or looks to find and specially as that very thing was not available earlier. On way, we did see many snow-capped peaks. At downhill we even faced thick fog and at places the visibility had become very low but only for a short while. The snow-capped peaks were really charming and enchanted us. The day was made. On way, KP Sir, as per his practice informed about arrival of our destination but somewhat late. On arrival after check-in some of us took tea, as we had taken lunch on way, in a wayside restauarant/dhaba but after ensuring that the service would be hygienic and fresh. It was a simple meal of Dal, Sabji, Salad, Pickle, Rice/Chapati and Curd. It was satisfactory arrangement. In Hotel NeelKanth we rested for a while and waited for the evening assembly.

The evening came, and after getting freshened up, we assembled around 7 p.m. The evening was as lively as always. The singing, drinks, as per choice, Namkeens of various types, and cucumber made it an

I have Resolved NOT to Stop

enjoyable affair. It was decided that the next day's departure would be again at 0830 hours, after early breakfast. The next day, after early tea and bath and breakfast, we packed our baggage for the next destination. Some snaps were taken. I could not desist from buying one Litre bottle of Malta Juice from that Restaurant/Hotel for Rs. 150/-, just to try out something different. We left almost on time. Brij Rani once again bought fresh Papaya and served us with her usual fervour. On way, Thapliyal bid goodbye, as he was to meet some relations but before departing, he informed from where to buy Bal Mithai (local sweet), which later on we could enjoy that evening, courtesy Neerja. Yes, of course we passed by Dhari Devi temple and bowed our heads in reverence.

On 4th October 2021, we left Hotel Neel Kanth almost on time. Here, it would not be out of place to mention that it was a simple and comfortable place, as there was no noise disturbance even from the nearby highway. The rooms were not decorated or carpeted but were of big size. Toilets also had twin-toilet facilities. There was no problem of water - hot or cold, but of course I noticed one thing over the trip that almost at every place, barring Hotel Him Shikhar in Chakori, the plumbing job needed better attention. Loose wash basin or leaking taps or pipes left a poor impression. Otherwise, even the linen was clean. The food served used to be freshly prepared and served as ordered.

With 2 pals M. Lal and Dr Suman Sharma

Dr. Suman Kumar Sharma was rather a shy and introvert person, but he used to enjoy every moment and indeed even got initiated into taking Beer. He used to sit next to me and always kept a happy disposition. As we had plenty of time to arrive at Chamba (another place than Chamba of Himachal Pradesh), our next night halt at Hotel Akash Lok, we kept slower pace and at every given moment, the snaps were taken and scenic beauty was enjoyed. We reached Tehri Dam, well in time. It was really a marvel spread over an area of 57 Sq. Kms. There was mention of many villages having been uprooted but the villagers were now benefiting from water, electricity and even employment. Of course, they had to leave their traditional homes and even occupations or even farming, but now there were better avenues. Development does cause initial problems and if it were not so there would have been no cars, trains, aircraft, spacecraft etc. On dam there was proper checking and strict instructions for not taking photographs. We saw Boating Arcade and noticed various types of boats going in the reservoir. We too got tempted and there was almost unanimous decision to try out. The hiring rates were high but perhaps essential for proper maintenance. Motorboat could take up to 13 persons and the charges were Rs. 500/- per person per hour. Speed boat was @ Rs. 1000/- for an hour. We also bought tickets and we were made to wear safety jackets. Perhaps, the police people could have been a little more imaginative, as they had put chairs and iron chains as barrier and for a person like me, it was difficult to cross over. They could have made a passage for people like me. But, perhaps, by their adopted way they could just sit and gossip. Of course, for me, the chairs were lowered to cross over. It indeed turned out to be an enjoyable ride and we covered the breadth of the reservoir and retuned taking a somewhat longer route.

Of course, singing and snapping continued. Some of us had even posed as one wished. KP Sir again informed hotel people that by what time to expect us and he also gave detailed instructions as what to prepare and the first thing he told was that as we were to reach there by 3 p.m. to prepare special Pakoras, Chutney, Wheat and Kuttu Chaptis and tea by 4 so that after wash we could munch something

I have Resolved NOT to Stop

Boating arcade at Tehri dam

and that evening meal could be enjoyed and of course even for the evening meal, there were strict instructions as what to prepare. The stress was on typical Garhwali Food and in that for evening tea, he had ordered Black Gram Pakoras to go along with Garlic, Mint, Coriander, Ginger, Tomatoes Chutney with fresh garlic leaves. Oh, yes, the Pakoras were really hot and mouthwatering. It was another highlight of the day.

In the Evening at 7 p.m. we again assembled to have drinks of our choice. I proposed a toast to compliment the contribution of KP Sir and everyone clapped and endorsed. For dinner, KP Sir had ordered Jhingore Ki Kheer (it is a kind of millet and even taken during fast); Raj Mah; Rai Ka Saag; and Sanso (mixed vegetable) with rice and Chapatis similar as were served earlier. Everyone praised the choice and enjoyed taste of freshly prepared meal. It turned out to be more in quantity than we actually required, and reason was dropping of two persons from original plans and the poor cook prepared for 11/12 persons, whereas, we had got reduced to 8 only (Satnam took his own meal, as usual; Thapliyal had left; and Dr Suman's wife had not joined though she was to come as per original plans).

We were to start around 9 a.m. the next morning so after enjoying immensely the evening we retired to our rooms and I for one had a sound sleep dreaming of greenery and snow-capped peaks. Yes, this

Uttarakhand - Holy and Wholesome at 78

Chamba is different than the one in Himachal Pradesh but no less beautiful and enjoyable.

Another very interesting thing, I recall. I had seen during uphill and downhill journeys a town, named, 'Narayan Bagad'. It seemed intriguing as normally the name of places after proper name end with 'Shahar'; or ' Nagar'; or 'Garh', or 'Pur" or even 'Aabad' but here the word 'Bagad', time and again came to my mind. When I checked with local people, it turned out to be a kind of 'Rice'. Of course, paddy in that area is aplenty. It made sense, meaning 'Narayan Variety or type of Rice'. But later on I was informed that Bagad was indeed a type of formation and had no connection with naming varieties of rice.

As KP Sir knew the late Mr. Naithani proprietor of Aakash Lok, he charged a very decent concessional rate. However, there arose a kind of misunderstanding with the cook for he charged for 12 persons instead of the 8 only present, on the plea that the original order was for 12 persons. He was of course paid, but it did leave a bad taste and KP Sir was much upset, about this episode. The cook, having cooked after having bought ingredients naturally did not want to suffer. So, he demanded full money. Since it was time to depart, the packed bags were stacked in the van.

Lest I forget, KP Sir, also gave me a copy of his book, "Safalata Ka Sangharsh" on previous evening. In fact, on his asking as to who reads Hindi literature, I had evinced interest, so he very graciously gave me his book. Since then, I have read it and found it to be written with heart and was as open as Mahatama Gandhi's "My Experiments with Truth". Simple and straight and no artificiality or effort to pretend.

On way, KP Sir did look for alternative places to stay in the future, which turned out to be either below par or costly. Ultimately, as he knew someone else, he arranged to see that camping site also. The place was called 'Namastay' in Kanatal. The actual camping place was nearly 1-1/2 Kms. from the main road and cars could go up to the place but it was not possible to take a van. The owner arranged to send a car, so a few of us led by KP Sir went to see the place. Not only he but others too liked the place, being nicely perched with orchards of almonds, walnuts and apples and moderately priced (Rs. 500 per person). Even the name was well coined giving meaning of 'Bowing in Hindi while Greeting" and Fine for Stay. There was also an open place to have a bonfire and thus, evening could be enjoyed jointly, talking and even presentation of cultural and artistic skills. Thumbs were up for next time.

Our next stop was Dhanaulti. Here we stopped to relieve ourselves, have tea and some of us took snacks or even freshly made Parathas. The tea and other preparations were good. Snaps were also taken. We could also see some places offering camping site, games and sports. On seeing fresh Bitter Gourds (Karelas), Brij Rani did not miss the opportunity to buy Karelas for self.

On way we came across a couple of streams but none matched to Kempty Falls in Mussoorie. At places snaps were taken and we came to Mussoorie's bypass to reach Dehradun. In Dehradun, the first to get down at hotel were Lal, Satnam and Brij Rani as that evening, they were to meet some other friends. I too was invited but I had to excuse myself to be able to see relations, like sister, brother-in-law and sister-in-law. The next KP Sir and the two ladies (leaving Neerja) got down. I was the next to say good-bye, as both Neerja and Dr. Suman were to get dropped off near Neeraj's place in Jolly Grant area.

I almost forgot to mention about Surkanda Devi Temple. It is a Shakti Peeth situated nearly 3 Kms from Kanatal and 2 Km of rough and tough climb from Kaddukhal. It is 3000 metres from sea level. The temple attracts many devotees. In fact. in Uttarakhand almost all villages have their Gram Devta's and there are also many famous temples of historical and religious importance all over Uttarakhand.

While on Uttarakhand tour, among other things, mention of Roorkee had come. It would not be out of place to elaborate a little more on that especially since as one advances in life, it is but natural that one would have many life experiences, memories of incidents, important events, anecdotes, etc. of childhood and early youth life. I was reminded by my younger brother that it was on 18th June 1955 (that was then 68 years ago) that we came to Roorkee by train from Kathgodam on the transfer of our father from Nainital, which we had left a day earlier in the morning by bus to cover 18 miles of bus journey up to Kathgodam. We passed through panoramic scenes of fields and

Uttarakhand - Holy and Wholesome at 78

ponds. However, when we reached Roorkee, it appeared to be a very small place, giving a forlorn look at the station. Father's friend was there to receive us, and we went on a Tonga to the place of our temporary stay. In about a fortnight, it was time to re-start schooling. Naturally, our father had to embark on the search for a suitable house close to school. Luckily, it was found in Ram Nagar, then popularly known as Beri Camp, where refugees from West Pakistan were given shelter and as the place was full of Ber trees, it was given that name - Ber tree is called Beri in Punjabi. My initial impression of Roorkee got changed, slowly but steadily, I started not only liking the place but almost falling in love with it and even today I admire Roorkee with fascination and am thankful for having spent my formative years there. Finally, I left Roorkee on 10th May, 1964 (Sunday) to come to Delhi and begin my forward journey in life.

I also recall that President Trump and earlier President Bill Clinton had visited India and went to see Taj Mahal in Agra but very few people may be able to recall that when President D. Eisenhower came to India in 1959 on first visit of any US President, among other things and visit to Taj, he visited Roorkee University. I distinctly recall this visit as that year I had also cleared my Matric. That was an honour for Roorkee University and rightly so.

Talking about my having cleared Matric, how can I forget to mention the school, KLDAV Intermediate School (Kanhaiya Lal Dayanand Anglo Vedic School). The founder of the school, Kanhaiya Lal had a great love for fruit trees. Believe me, close to the main entrance, there were trees of Ber (Plum), which were most probably wild. Of course, close to entrance there was Anwla Tree and of course another peculiar tree was Maulashree with fragrance and tiny fruits close to his own cottage and Library. More importantly, there were dozens of Mango trees in the compound near our classrooms. Flower plants of different varieties used to adorn the morning assembly area. There were good laboratories for practicals in Chemistry, Physics and Biology. There used to be two sessions of school: the first of junior classes, from 6th to 8th and later on for 9th to 12th. Later on, a degree College was also added but in a separate building. There was a huge playground. Of course, there was another mango garden with hundreds of fruit trees including of other fruits, like Locat, Leechis, Guvava, etc. Mangoes were of different varieties but all of them produced sweet mangoes. We not only used to play on trees but would also sneak in these gardens during fruit season. It was true that fruit crop was auctioned and there were caretakers during the season but then there used to be boyish pranks and see-saw battle between them and a few daredevils. The temptation was always greater than possible scolding or even punishment of cane thrashing.

Sports were not overlooked. In the evenings football, hockey were common. The school produced some good district and even state level athletes. There was a good cricket team also. It was during cricket games that I was exposed to the habit of listening commentaries on Radio. Yes, the school also arranged picnics, scouting, ACC and NCC drills. Other important arms of complete education system, like debates, art competition, poem recitation and dramatics were also not overlooked. Writing in school magazine also helped in improving writing skills. The school ensured teaching staff of all communities and of course they were all devoted to their duties and always helpful even beyond school hours. Many of us joined Roorkee University after completing Intermediate or even later. Some joined Army or became doctors or joined and excelled in other professions or even business. In moulding me, yes, of course, the school played an important role. I used to take part enthusiastically in various activities. After completing Intermediate from there in 1961, I preferred, Arts side instead of science side, though much against the wishes of my father and to his disappointment but I knew my weakness of not being able to grasp Maths, much essential for Science Stream. It proved a boon in disguise, as I was able to devote myself where my heart was, and which provided me opportunity to see and serve various parts of the world. But I must admit that KLDAV School helped me a lot in bringing out best in me. I do not know as to how many of us of that time are still in existence and no less as to how many of them share and endorse my thoughts.

A couple of years ago, clean cities of India were announced. In Uttaranchal, only Roorkee found its name in that list. While without negating the efforts which Roorkee Municipal authorities must have put in to keep city clean, a great credit deservedly must go to areas of

Cantt, IIT Roorkee, CBRI and Irrigation Research Institute which have been keeping their sprawling complexes, literally, adjacent to each other clean. These areas have a lot of trees, lawns, gardens and were well kept. In any case, Cantonments are known to be cleaner parts of any city. Since, I had a childhood association with the city, many memories became fresh. When we came to Roorkee in 1956, It was then a Tehsil of District Saharanpur and Hardwar was its part as a Pargana. Later on, Hardwar was declared as a District and Roorkee became its Tehsil, by Mayawati Government and on formation of Uttarakhand (Uttaranchal) it then became part of Uttarakhand. Roorkee has certain geographical peculiarities and the traditional city of Roorkee was a minor part of Roorkee area, as major portion used to be covered by Cantonment area (being Headquarters of Bengal Engineering Group), IIT Roorkee (earlier known as Thomson College and University of Roorkee and established more than 175 years ago) - the premier institution in Asia of Civil Engineering), other institutions, both central and state, like Central Building Research Institute (CBRI), Structural Research Institute, Seismography Institute and Irrigation Research Institute.

Two water bodies - Upper Ganges Canal pass through the city and Saloni, a rainy river forms boundary of a good part of Roorkee town. Another rainy river, Dhanouri was only six miles from Roorkee. The canal is an engineering marvel and having been built in 19th century makes really one wonder. It was supposed to be the only canal boasting 3 miles of Pucca Ghats. At Ranipur one rainy river has been channeled to pass over it. At Dhanouri, the river and canal cross and the Saloni River flows under it near Roorkee. The canal is also used to generate hydroelectricity, apart from irrigation.

Piran Kaliar, one of the three Sufi pilgrimage is close by and is supposed to be the site of first rail in India, used for carrying material for building canal. The snow-capped hills of Mussoorie were something one could see in those days, when pollution was rare. The holy city of Hardwar was also close by, and we used to venture there on our bikes.

Coming on trees, Roorkee also used to have a lot of Jamun, Guava and Litchi trees. Ponds in and around Roorkee used to produce

Chestnuts. On one side of Roorkee- Hardwar Road, there used to be a lot of coconut trees. Its leaves used to provide raw material for making hand fans and other kitchen items, like Chapati Keeper., brooms etc. I recall a Muslim artisan engaging himself in making Khaki Jungle Hats for which the main materials used were: Khaki Cloth and Sarkandas (A kind of wild grow cane grass and on peeling its stems one would find white cork type stuff, which was used to make the frame of hats).

So far as religious composition of Roorkee in those days was concerned, Hindus, Muslims, Jains, Sikhs and Christians used to live harmoniously. The city would have many cultural programmes, from Ram Leela, local fairs to the annual Ur's in Piran Kaliyar. Dancing girls from various parts used to come and would pitch their tents. Religion and revelry would go on smoothly side by side. Of course, Hardwar used to have fairs and religious congregations, like of Kumbh, Ganga Snan (Dips), which Roorkee canal also used to have but at much smaller scale. Local fairs, like Ghughal ka Mela, used to attract many from nearby villages. On Diwali, display of illumination by some biggies, I would compare with illumination on Christmas for competition in some US cities. The festival of Holi used to see bazar streets coloured with Tesu water. Cantt Gurudwara's Guru Parab used to attract a lot many people from far off places. Roorkee in those days also used to organize many other cultural events, like Kavi Sammelans, Mushairas, Quawwali Nights, staging of dramas etc. There used to be always endless fun in one form or the other, like picnics, scouting, visit to Flower Valley. The Reading Room of Municipal Commitee also had well-stocked Library, which provided me good opportunity to read many a classics. Roorkee had well spread cottage industry of Drawing Boards from Kail Wood and Drawing and Measurement Instruments for engineering education.

How can I forget mentioning that in 1960s, Thakur Yashpal Singh of village Paniala became MP (Independent) from this place after defeating the then Irrigation Minister in UP Government, Hazi Ibrahim. I am mentioning him for his peculiar style of living. He would come to city turbaned on a horseback. With his big mustache, he used to impress many. He used to live in a world of fantasy and was capable of taking many with him. I believe it was composite culture of Roorkee, which helped many of us to shape ourselves to withstand in this world!

First, on purpose, I had not mentioned in my write-up earlier about a couple of things I had bought from Chamba (UK) on the suggestion of KP Sir, when with all his seriousness, he told me to buy a few more things to promote local artisans as also to carry something unique and as memory of Uttarakhand trip. I bought (1) Rope, hand-knit which is used to tie domesticated animals; (2) A bell which adorns animal neck and announces arrival of animal; (3) Hansyia; and (4) Kudal to tend my garden. Even my daughter, Surabhi, found them useful, so I had shared something with her. Love for local produces also made me to request the Cook of Aakash Lok to give me a little sample of rice/millet used to prepare Kheer the previous night. He had dutifully made a small packet, as sample and one day, I am going to buy some more of it and try my hand at Kheer of Uttarakhand. We of course returned to our home on 6th evening by train and dutifully my daughter, son-in-law (Pawan) and granddaughter were at the Railway Station to welcome us back though it was quite late in the evening. I must add here that when our train had started running from Ghaziabad, a person from our compartment itself had accidentally dropped his mobile outside and he pulled chain. The train had to be stopped to carry out formalities and the train again went ahead some distance and again stopped so that the mobile could be picked up. Naturally, in the process the train got late by a few minutes. These the were, of course, vagaries of modern-day gadgetry and travel.

I have Resolved NOT to Stop

Hansiya and Kudal as mementos from Chamba, Uttarakhand

In short, it was one of the most economical, educational and wholly entertaining trip and such trips could be repeated with minor alterations about such a venture was going to be a permanent fixture. I do hope that your reading journey was almost equally enjoyable as mine in realty and you are satisfied with the unfolded reel. Moreover, it would have created some zeal in you to follow my example of No Stop!

Epilogue

I am tempted to write a few lines to share that I have experienced that the habit of frequent travel or outings has inculcated certain traits in me, besides being life-long memory and life-time experiences, addition to my knowledge firsthand of various territories and people, scenic beauty of various places present, customs and lives of various people in different parts, as also how to be a practical and a safe traveller. I check when it would be best to travel to a place, keeping weather in mind. I am also able to equip myself in most efficient manner to withstand possible difficulties likely to be encountered. Travel regulations, including prohibition like restrictions are also kept in mind. I also do not abhor trying something new and always try to keep my adventure spirit ignited. I also found that I was able to get most open and candid reactions of people, like a Reporter, from people with whom I interacted in person in private conversations and especially as each one of them knew I was neither a cameraman nor a reporter, so opening up natural and neutral. No less important is the fact that I find myself both physically and mentally fitter than before, for which I recall a common saying in Hindi, 'Aam Ke Aam, Guthliyon Ke Dam'. Killing two birds with one stone, though I mean no harm to any innocent creature and that too tiny, harmless and innocent birds, which nature has given us to enjoy their chirping sounds.

I must also thank my friends and well-wishers who had encouraged to embark on this venture and share with more people my experiences. I am grateful for their well-intended advice to benefit as many people as possible.

I also assure my ardent readers that if encouraged by them, I shall definitely come out with my international travels and other experiences.

I have Resolved NOT to Stop

I am confident that readers would like to get some insight of my experiences of different countries, having different environments, geography, flora, and fauna and even regimes from Monarchy to Communism. I shall therefore be well advised and encouraged by positive response. In the meantime, please enjoy and do not forget to write to me with any suggestions for any improvement, wherever necessary.

As I have resolved not to stop, I do hope that some motivation must have been created among readers. Also, I do not claim it to be a Work of Literature but have merely put in it my feelings as a common old man for common people. As it is said "Heart to Heart" without any artificial flavour and I have tried to be factually correct and honest in my effort. My readers may be the judge whether it has actually created the desire to Try it yourself and that is the simple aim.

www.ingramcontent.com/pod-product-compliance
Lightning Source LLC
Chambersburg PA
CBHW061925240825
31572CB00022BA/1259